The Magic Presence™

THE ASCENDED MASTERS
SPEAK ON ANGELS

"I AM" ACTIVITY

OF

SAINT GERMAIN FOUNDATION

The "I AM" Activity represents the Original, Permanent, and Highest Source of the Ascended Masters' Instruction on the Great Laws of Life, as first offered to the western world by the Ascended Master Saint Germain, through His Accredited Messengers, Mr. and Mrs. Guy W. Ballard.

In the early 1930s the Ballards established Saint Germain Foundation and Saint Germain Press, Inc., which under Saint Germain's Guidance, have expanded into world-wide organizations that offer to mankind the true Ascended Master Teachings on the Great Cosmic Words, "I AM"! Saint Germain Foundation strives to keep the "I AM" Ascended Master Instruction in Its pure, unadulterated form, free from any human interpretation, personal monetary gain, or proselytizing, as It is a Gift from the Great Ascended Masters and Cosmic Beings to bring Illumination and Perfection to mankind.

Hundreds of "I AM" Temples and Sanctuaries exist throughout the world, where the Teachings are applied in "I AM" Decree Groups. The Books of the Saint Germain Series are available in many libraries, bookstores, or directly from Saint Germain Press (address below). For further information, please contact:

SAINT GERMAIN FOUNDATION
SAINT GERMAIN PRESS
1120 Stonehedge Drive
Schaumburg, Illinois 60194 USA
(847) 882-7400 or (800) 662-2800
www.saintgermainfoundation.org
www.saintgermainpress.com

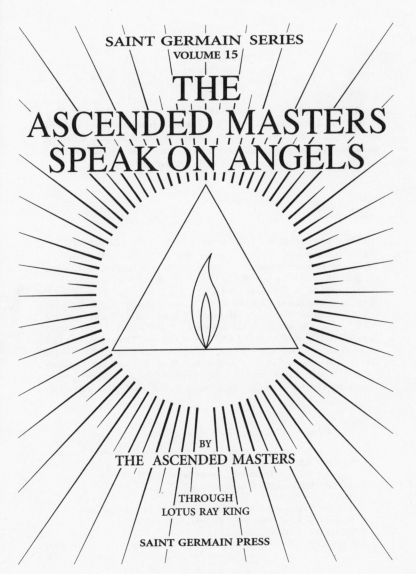

SAINT GERMAIN SERIES
VOLUME 15

THE
ASCENDED MASTERS
SPEAK ON ANGELS

BY
THE ASCENDED MASTERS

THROUGH
LOTUS RAY KING

SAINT GERMAIN PRESS

3/03 *   *   *

TRADEMARKS AND SERVICE MARKS OF SAINT GERMAIN FOUNDATION INCLUDE: The Ascended Masters Instruction on the "Beloved Mighty I AM Presence,"* The Ascended Masters' Instruction,ˢᴹ "Beloved Mighty I AM Presence,"* Daughters of Light,* Heart of Heaven,ˢᴹ Honor Cross,* Honor Cross Design,* "I AM",* "I AM" Activity,* "I AM" Angels of Light,* "I AM" Ascended Master Youth,ˢᴹ "I AM" Ascended Master Youth Newsletter,* "I AM" COME!* "I AM" Emblem,* "I AM" Music of the Spheres,* "I AM" Reading Room,* "I AM" Religious Activity,* "I AM" Religious Broadcast,* "I AM" Sanctuary,* "I AM" School,* "I AM" Student Body,* "I AM" Study Groups,* "I AM" Temple,* "I AM" University,ˢᴹ "I AM" Violet Flame,™ The Magic Presence,™ "Mighty I AM Presence," ˢᴹ Minute Men of Saint Germain,* Music of the Spheres,* Saint Germain,* Saint Germain's Pantry,ˢᴹ Saint Germain Foundation,* Saint Germain Press, Inc.,* Shasta Springs,* Unfed Flame Design,* Violet Consuming Flame,* Violet Flame,* "Voice of the I AM"*

Library of Congress Cataloging-in-Publication Data

The ascended masters speak on angels / by the ascended masters through Lotus Ray King.
       p.   cm. -- (The Saint Germain series ; v. 15)
    Includes bibliographical references.
    ISBN 1-878891-65-0
    1. I AM Religious Activity--Doctrines.2. Angels--Miscellanea.
I. King, Lotus Ray, 1886-1971. II. Series.
BP605.I18A84   1998
299' .93—dc21

                                                            98-51057
                                                            CIP

CONTENTS

ONE-COLOR PICTURES

DEDICATION

his Series of Books is dedicated in deepest Eternal Love and Gratitude to our Beloved Ascended Masters, Beloved Saint Germain, Beloved Jesus, Beloved Godfre and Lotus, Beloved Nada and the Great Divine Director, the Great Host of Ascended Masters, the Great Cosmic Beings, and especially Beloved Archangel Michael, the Angel Deva from the Jade Temple, the Great Listening Angel, the Great Cosmic Angel on whose Crown blazes the Word Union, and the Great Angelic Host whose Presence on this Earth has blessed us throughout the centuries in ways not recognized by the mankind of this world.

The Dictations in this Book were given through our Beloved Accredited Messenger, Mrs. G. W. Ballard, whose pen name is Lotus Ray King. We thank and bless Her for being the Open Door through which this Knowledge of the Ascended Masters and the Great Angelic Host could be presented to mankind.

As you read these Words, may you enter into the Conscious Awareness of what the Angelic Host will do and can do as soon as you accept Their Presence, and live, move, and have your being in the remembrance of the Love which They pour at your Call, and which They bring by Their very Presence which you acknowledge. You cannot acknowledge anything about the Angelic Host and not have immediately the Victory of Their Love flow in and around you as a Flame from Their Hearts.

TRIBUTE

his Tribute to the Great Angelic Host is made with all the gratitude of our Hearts for Their existence in this Universe. To the various Angels, always with us, but whom we had forgotten for so long, we welcome You in the Name of the "Beloved Mighty I AM Presence" and the Great Host of Ascended Masters. We salute You with the sign of the Heart, Head, and Hand. We accept You into the physical action of our daily lives as we give conscious recognition to You, now and forever!

Beloved Archangel Michael says: "Sometimes you know, it takes a great deal of Patience for Us to wait upon wayward humanity year after year, after they've been given the Pearls of Existence on a golden platter—just wait until they get through following their own experiment with misery! I am speaking of this tonight because the *conscious under-standing* of what the Angelic Host do to assist mankind must come to the intellect of human beings who are intelligent enough to understand It.

"If I were you who abide within this city [Los Angeles], I certainly would not let the day go by that I did not give love and gratitude and recognition to all of the Angelic Host who have ministered here in the past, who guard your Destiny of the future, and who abide with you in the present. These are Friends to Life. The Angelic Host are Guardians of good. They are the Masters and the Victorious Presence of Love— Love that mankind understands as yet very little of Its Blessings to Life. And all of that is waiting, waiting, waiting for recognition, for acceptance, for use, and for your Call, that it may come into physical conditions and manifest Its Control and Transmuting Love to raise those conditions into the Perfection of Our Octave.

"So Beloved Ones, when you realize how wonderful these Great Beings are, and how many Ascended Masters and Cosmic Beings—and those of the Angelic Host—are ever ministering to the people of this world, and ever awaiting an opening and an opportunity to give only the Blessings that bring Happiness to all; and yet mankind go on oblivious of Their Divine Presence, simply because their attention is occupied with their own desires. I am drawing forth from within you the latent memory of the Reality of the Angelic Host and of some of Their Blessings that you have received in the centuries past. There isn't a one in this room tonight who hasn't in the past had some conscious contact with the Angelic Host, through which was received Divine Assistance of Transcendent Power!

"Now I would be very grateful if you would call for the Authority of the Angelic Host in the Miracle Love which They send to this Earth, to charge forth into the desires of the feeling world of mankind, and see if We cannot awaken the Eternal, Divine Desire within the feeling world to become like the Angels. MANKIND, O MAN-KIND! AWAKEN TONIGHT TO THE DIVINE BEINGS WHO HOLD THEIR HANDS OUT TO YOU FOR ASSISTANCE, WHO HAVE POURED LOVE THROUGH THE AGES, WHO STAND AWAITING THE OPPORTUNITY TO CONSUME LIKE A SCROLL IN THE HEAV-ENS THE UNFORTUNATE CREATION THAT SELFISHNESS HAS IMPOSED UPON GOD'S UNIVERSE! We would appreciate a Decree that would compel mankind to awaken to the Real-ity of the Angelic Host, to the Understanding of Their Service, and to some Gratitude to that

Divine Life that has blessed them and always blesses them so greatly from the Octaves above.

"There are Uncountable Legions of Angels whose Love would make you weep with Joy, were you to see Their Approach at your Call. So often mankind have thought the Guardian Angels were only for children—and it just happens that all mankind are children! So since it is My Privilege to wield certain Authority in the Awakening of mankind to that which the Angelic Host are about to do, I am pleading for My Friends! I trust you will accept Them as *your Friends!*"

Record CD 1826; Cassette 60198; September 1, 1953

These Dictations were recorded during Saint Germain Foundation Classes of the "I AM" Activity in various parts of the United States of America between the years 1950 through 1966. The Dictations are arranged in chronological order. Some of the Dictations are totally on the subject of Angels. Some have varied subject matter, but contain sections in which special qualities or activities of the Angelic Host are presented for the first time to the reader. All of the Dictations are previously unpublished, and

Saint Germain Foundation is pleased to offer lovingly this Ascended Master Knowledge of Angels to the Student Body and the world.

"I AM" OUR CALL TO THE ANGELS

"I AM" Angels and Angels and Angels!
Legions of Angels of Love!
"I AM" Angels and Angels and Angels!
Legions of Angels above!
"I AM" Angels and Angels and Angels!
Legions of Angels draw nigh!
"I AM" Angels and Angels and Angels!
Legions of Angels stand by!

"I AM" Angels and Angels and Angels!
Angels of Violet Flame!
"I AM" Angels and Angels and Angels!
Singing the Song of God's Name!
"I AM" Angels and Angels and Angels!
Of Music and Peace of the Spheres!
"I AM" Angels and Angels and Angels!
Of Healing—the Song each Heart hears!

"I AM" Angels and Angels and Angels!
Bring Love! Their Glory "I AM"!

(continued)

"I AM" Angels and Angels and Angels!
  Are speaking God's Great Command!
"I AM" Angels and Angels and Angels!
  Of Flame and Cosmic Christ Light!
"I AM" Angels and Angels and Angels!
  Pouring to us God's Great Might!

"I AM" Angels and Angels and Angels!
  Of God—the "Almighty I AM"!
"I AM" Angels and Angels and Angels!
  In Legions around us stand!
"I AM" Angels and Angels and Angels!
  Of Power from God's Cosmic Height!
"I AM" Angels and Angels and Angels!
  Are bringing us Victory's Might!

"I AM" Angels and Angels and Angels!
  In Limitless Legions descend!
"I AM" Angels and Angels and Angels!
  All of our loved ones defend!
"I AM" Angels and Angels and Angels!
  Protecting now stand by us all!
"I AM" Angels and Angels and Angels!
  Fulfill each instant our Call!

(continued)

"I AM" Oceans and Oceans and Oceans
   Of Victory's Flame everywhere!
"I AM" Oceans and Oceans and Oceans
   Of God's Great, Great Loving Care!
"I AM" Oceans and Oceans and Oceans
   Of all Wealth from God's Heart and Hand!
"I AM" Oceans and Oceans and Oceans
   Of God's Heart's Flame, and in It I stand!

"I AM" Oceans and Oceans and Oceans
   Of God's Music of all the Spheres!
"I AM" Oceans and Oceans and Oceans
   Of Healing as Earth It clears!
"I AM" Oceans and Oceans and Oceans
   Of God's Flame that purifies all!
"I AM" Oceans and Oceans and Oceans
   Of Victory in our every Call!

"I AM" Oceans and Oceans and Oceans
   Of Power! OBEDIENCE "I AM"!
"I AM" Oceans and Oceans and Oceans
   Of Wisdom in every Command!
"I AM" Oceans and Oceans and Oceans
   Of Harmony's Song of the Light!

(continued)

"I AM" Oceans and Oceans and Oceans
    Of Justice from Love's Cosmic Height!

"I AM" Oceans and Oceans and Oceans
    Of such Power as none have seen!
"I AM" Oceans and Oceans and Oceans
    Of God on whose "Presence" I lean!
"I AM" Oceans and Oceans and Oceans
    Of such Love as has never been known!
"I AM" Oceans and Oceans and Oceans
    Of Silence and Love—God's Heart Tone!

"I AM" Oceans and Oceans and Oceans
    Of the Sound of God's Cosmic Voice!
"I AM" Oceans and Oceans and Oceans
    Of God's Words which make all rejoice!
"I AM" Oceans and Oceans and Oceans
    Of Beauty and Youth and of Health!
"I AM" Oceans and Oceans and Oceans
    Of God's Life—THE GREATEST OF
    WEALTH!

                    Chanera
            "Voice of the I AM" July, 1946

"I AM" ANGELS

"I AM" Thousands and Thousands and Thousands
    Of Angels in Oceans of Flame!
"I AM" Thousands and Thousands and Thousands
    Of Angels now speaking God's Name!
"I AM" Thousands and Thousands and Thousands
    Of Angels of Music and Song!
"I AM" Thousands and Thousands and Thousands
    Of Angels correcting each wrong!

"I AM" Legions and Legions and Legions
    Of Angels now flooding the Earth!
"I AM" Legions and Legions and Legions
    Of Angels and Earth's Cosmic Birth!
"I AM" Legions and Legions and Legions
    Of Angels of Victory's Might!
"I AM" Legions and Legions and Legions
    Of Angels here! Blazing God's Light!

"I AM" Oceans and Oceans and Oceans
    Of Flame which those Angels now bring!
"I AM" Oceans and Oceans and Oceans
    Of Peace in the Song that They sing!

"I AM" Oceans and Oceans and Oceans
    Of the Blessings and Gifts They give!
"I AM" Oceans and Oceans and Oceans
    Of God's Freedom in which They live!

"I AM" Oceans and Oceans and Oceans
    Of the Sound of God's Cosmic Voice!
"I AM" Oceans and Oceans and Oceans
    Of God's Miracles—Come! Now! Rejoice!
"I AM" Oceans and Oceans and Oceans
    Of Power from God's Cosmic Heart!
"I AM" Oceans and Oceans and Oceans
    Of Love that can never depart!

"I AM" Oceans and Oceans and Oceans
    Of Truth that Freedom may live!
"I AM" Oceans and Oceans and Oceans
    Of Healing I love to give!
"I AM" Oceans and Oceans and Oceans
    Of Protection by God's Great Might!
"I AM" Oceans and Oceans and Oceans
    Of Perfection and Miracles of Light!

"I AM" Angels and Angels and Angels!
    Heal instantly at our Command!

(continued)

"I AM" Angels and Angels and Angels!
Compel Perfection at hand!
"I AM" Angels and Angels and Angels!
Bring Gifts that only They give!
"I AM" Angels and Angels and Angels!
Are present wherever we live!

"I AM" Angels and Angels and Angels!
Bring wealth from Octaves above!
"I AM" Angels and Angels and Angels!
Control wherever we move!
"I AM" Angels and Angels and Angels!
Clear all before us each day!
"I AM" Angels and Angels and Angels!
Flood Love and forever hold sway!

"I AM" Angels and Angels and Angels!
Singing as only They can!
"I AM" Angels and Angels and Angels!
We see and in Their Flame stand!
"I AM" Angels and Angels and Angels!
Around us in Legions all see!
"I AM" Angels and Angels and Angels!
Compel us Eternally Free!

Chanera

"Voice of the I AM" July, 1946

CHAPTER I

GODDESS OF LIGHT

Chicago, Illinois
April 10, 1950
Record CD 1336

Beloved of the Light, in the Radiance which We are bringing tonight, I wish to remind you of your tremendous privilege in the use of the Cosmic Light; and I wish to thank you for everything—every Call you have ever made that helps Us to accomplish that which must be done in preventing mankind from going into any further destruction. You hardly have realized, Beloved Ones, what the Cosmic Light means to you all, and how It is released under your direction at your Call.

Not in any cycle of time in the past has the Cosmic Law permitted the Release of that Cosmic Light Substance from Our Octave of Life, because in drawing It into the lower atmosphere of Earth, It energizes everything in the entire atmosphere of Earth. Mankind in the past, because of their frightful destructive accumulation, were not permitted to draw the Cosmic Energy into outer use such as you are doing today by your Calls for the Cosmic Light. And My Sister, the Goddess of Liberty, is one who was responsible—with Myself—for determining to go to the Great Central Sun and ask for the Release of this Power, at least to those who came under the Mighty Saint Germain's Direction.

What the outer world calls the Cosmic Rays is not the Power that We direct which you know of as the Cosmic Light. The Cosmic Light Substance which comes forth at your Call, My Dear Ones, is the Direct Radiation of Light Substance from the Ascended Masters in the Great Central Sun, and that is not the same as the Great Universal Light Substance which mankind know of as the universal energy that fills all space. The Cosmic Light Substance which comes forth at your Call, under Our Direction, is that which is drawn forth and qualified with the Consciousness and Perfection of the Great Cosmic Beings in the Central Sun who give that of Their own volition. It is the actual Radiation from Their own Life

Streams, concentrated, qualified, and directed to do certain definite Work wherever It passes by. Therefore as It comes into the atmosphere of Earth and locates, so the people get the benefit of It, they absorb that—they breathe It in as you breathe in oxygen through the lungs. And as that Fire enters into their mentality, into the mental and feeling world, It compels a certain amount of Illumination to come to the consciousness of the mass of the people.

This is a Lifting Power to the whole of mankind. It also increases the vibratory action tremendously of the Powers of Nature, and even into the atmosphere of Earth. It is not what you call the air you breathe. That is of an intensity that is adjusted to your atomic structure; but the Cosmic Light Substance that enters into the mental and feeling world of mankind absolutely annihilates wrong thoughts and wrong feelings and, as it were, draws the Life Flame and the constructive impulses from within the outer self into greater action, and fans that until it expands and holds the balance against destructive forces.

Thank you for your Decree tonight for the White Fire of the Cosmic Light to come forth everywhere within the Nation and fire the people awake and blast them free; for It does exactly that thing in their mental and feeling world—and Heaven knows, they need It! I'll tell you, there shall come forth such Light in the brain structure of mankind, there shall come forth such Light in this government as shall compel destructive forces to fear longer to continue their destructive plans! You have no idea the degradation which they plan for you; and I tell you, if the American people knew their intent, if they knew the way and means that they would adopt, there isn't a person within your borders who is constructive who wouldn't arise and wipe out everything that seeks to destroy them! My Dear Ones, if you don't arise and wipe them out, they'll wipe you out! And aren't you more important on the Earth than the destructive forces? *(applause)* Thank you so much, Precious Ones. Please be seated.

Now remember this: Everything that is of war, everything that is of communism, everything that is of the beast of destruction is criminal insanity. And certainly you wouldn't give any quarter to that if it were acting through an individual. If the mind had completely gone off, and the feelings had become wholly destructive, you surely wouldn't hesitate to leash that body and keep it atmosphere of Earth, or make the Call for It until It becomes physically visible to all. And there are ways and means of making mankind understand when they become so hard that they won't listen to reason. And that's what is needed at the moment! Were you to see as We do the Magnificent Light in many Life Streams of the Younger Generation, and all of that delayed or shut off because they drive them to drink and depravity in a few years—O Dear Ones, it's tragic beyond expression! And I am determined, just as determined, to dissolve that stuff from the Universe that has so depraved mankind, as I was to remove the black magicians! And thanks to you, it has been done! *(applause)* Thank you, Precious Ones.

And while you are standing, may I ask you to send forth your Call, and demand that the Cosmic Christ Legions of Cosmic Blue Flame sweep into the lower atmosphere of Earth and take Their Cosmic Toll in the beast of the world! Use those Words! And when I speak of that beast, it not only the war beast, but it's all its claws! But you ask for those Cosmic Christ Legions of Cosmic Blue Flame to sweep everywhere in the er physical atmosphere of Earth, and take

from injuring others, would you? Well, there's no difference between the mass accumulation of the communists and the war element than there would be in a criminally insane individual. That is but a mass accumulation of many. So please don't allow the slightest feeling of lethargy to enter into your world at all, and don't allow any false sympathy to get hold of you! I'm warning you tonight because the forces of depravity are subtle in the extreme, and they don't miss an instant to connect you or your energy with something destructive if they can get your attention!

Now you, on the other hand, mustn't miss a moment of keeping yourselves connected with your "Presence," with the Ascended Host, and of eating, sleeping, and breathing your connection with your "Presence" and the Source of Perfection. Those are the forces suggested to mankind constantly—subtle means by which they gain the attention, and the next thing you know, evil has driven in. You must use your Conscious Understanding to command the outer attention of yourselves and others to be held to that "Mighty I AM Presence," to accept the Ascended Host, to see Their Manifestations, to understand Their

Power, and know from whence comes the Help that offsets the destructive forces. And I for one know well enough their treachery and their subtle means of trapping individuals who are almost Free!

That's the reason I have come tonight—to make this clear to all of you, so you don't allow any false sympathy of any kind to enter in and imagine that these individuals have anything in their plans except enslaving you and degrading anything that is God-like or constructive. Remember this, for all that they call it—a world government—they do not have that back of their motive. Their motive is to destroy everything, and make no mistake about it! And if you imagine there is anything good in that kind of a government, you don't know the ABC's of Wisdom!

Now don't allow any sympathy or any acceptance of any argument in their favor. I have come to give this Warning, because some of the Students have been asleep in their feelings and imagined that these forces are not as vicious as they seem. They're far more so than you see on the surface, and I happen to know, because I have dealt with them! I'm here to protect you,

and since you have made that Call for the White Fire Substance of the Cosmic Light to come forth everywhere within the Nation and fire the people awake and blast them Free, your one Decree tonight has opened the Door to enable Me to act in certain capacity that will bless you and your Nation forever! *(applause)* Thank you, Precious Ones, with all My Heart. We shall amplify that with Power that the destructive forces shall know and understand and feel! Thank you! Won't you be seated, please.

Now remember this, and please remind yourselves often, when you call for a thing, you responding and giving obedience to the scious Command of Life—and the Con Instruction that has been given to m through the centuries, "CALL UNTO M I WILL ANSWER THEE!" You have Loved Ones, and the Answer is as su fest as that the Sun exists in the Hea you tonight! This is My own Perso to you, because it enables Us to the Outpouring of that Cosmic which must come if mankind

Stand your ground! Be draw the White Fire of the C

their Cosmic Toll in the beast of the world! The liquor and dope beast and other channels shall die as they should! *(applause)* Thank you, Precious Ones.

I want to reveal to you that the third one who went to the Great Central Sun with the Beloved Goddess of Liberty and Myself was **the Great Cosmic Angel on whose Crown blazes the Word "Union"**! *(applause)* Beloved Ones, I'm revealing to you tonight certain Inner Actions of the Law concerning your Nation. **The Goddess of Liberty and the Cosmic Angel with Myself have taken the Responsibility of removing the liquor beast and those destructive cravings from the emotional bodies of this Nation, and that's not a light task!** *(applause)* Thank you, Beloved Ones.

When you realize the creations in the emotional bodies of the people who are caught in that beast's destructive activity—the beast of war and all its claws—those creations are frightful to behold! But I tell you that when the Legions, the Cosmic Christ Legions of Cosmic Christ Blue Flame approach those beasts, their terror is worse—and they are to face that by My Command! *(applause)* Thank you. Their torture, their

depravity, and their destruction has been frightful and inexcusable, and they must be annihilated
from the Universe. And I shall appreciate, as
well as the Beloved Goddess of Justice, and this
Mighty Cosmic Angel who came to Washington—We shall appreciate every ounce of energy
you give, every Call you make, until that condition is removed from the Universe, and its record
blasted from Life. It must be done! There is no
hope for mankind's Freedom until those frightful things are withdrawn and placed in the Violet-blue Flame where they cannot exist longer.

Therefore My Gratitude to you is boundless.
And may I say to you, the hour when those
things are removed, and the mankind of Earth
feels the release from those frightful torturing
cravings, will your gratitude and your love know
what it means to stand to the Light and carry It
high—until those in the darkness are drawn back
Home into the Heart of that which is Eternal
Happiness. And when you see those Life Streams
one by one coming back to the condition in
which is their Divine Birthright, you will know
as We do that it's worth every effort you would
ever make to compel those forces into annihilation. And you will be grateful with all you are

from injuring others, would you? Well, there's no difference between the mass accumulation of the communists and the war element than there would be in a criminally insane individual. That is but a mass accumulation of many. So please don't allow the slightest feeling of lethargy to enter into your world at all, and don't allow any false sympathy to get hold of you! I'm warning you tonight because the forces of depravity are subtle in the extreme, and they don't miss an instant to connect you or your energy with something destructive if they can get your attention!

Now you, on the other hand, mustn't miss a moment of keeping yourselves connected with your "Presence," with the Ascended Host, and of eating, sleeping, and breathing your connection with your "Presence" and the Source of Perfection. Those are the forces suggested to mankind constantly—subtle means by which they gain the attention, and the next thing you know, evil has driven in. You must use your Conscious Understanding to command the outer attention of yourselves and others to be held to that "Mighty I AM Presence," to accept the Ascended Host, to see Their Manifestations, to understand Their

Power, and know from whence comes the Help that offsets the destructive forces. And I for one know well enough their treachery and their subtle means of trapping individuals who are almost Free!

That's the reason I have come tonight—to make this clear to all of you, so you don't allow any false sympathy of any kind to enter in and imagine that these individuals have anything in their plans except enslaving you and degrading anything that is God-like or constructive. Remember this, for all that they call it—a world government—they do not have that back of their motive. Their motive is to destroy everything, and make no mistake about it! And if you imagine there is anything good in that kind of a government, you don't know the ABC's of Wisdom!

Now don't allow any sympathy or any acceptance of any argument in their favor. I have come to give this Warning, because some of the Students have been asleep in their feelings and imagined that these forces are not as vicious as they seem. They're far more so than you see on the surface, and I happen to know, because I have dealt with them! I'm here to protect you, and since you have made that Call for the White Fire Substance of the Cosmic Light to come forth everywhere within the Nation and fire the people awake and blast them Free, your one Decree tonight has opened the Door to enable Me to act in certain capacity that will bless you and your Nation forever! *(applause)* Thank you, Precious Ones, with all My Heart. We shall amplify that with Power that the destructive forces shall know and understand and feel! Thank you! Won't you be seated, please.

Now remember this, and please remind yourselves often, when you call for a thing, you are responding and giving obedience to the Conscious Command of Life—and the Conscious Instruction that has been given to mankind through the centuries, "CALL UNTO ME AND I WILL ANSWER THEE!" You have called, My Loved Ones, and the Answer is as sure to manifest as that the Sun exists in the Heavens! Thank you tonight! This is My own Personal Gratitude to you, because it enables Us to again increase the Outpouring of that Cosmic Light Substance which must come if mankind are to have Help.

Stand your ground! Be adamant—but you draw the White Fire of the Cosmic Light into the atmosphere of Earth, or make the Call for It until It becomes physically visible to all. And there are ways and means of making mankind understand when they become so hard that they won't listen to reason. And that's what is needed at the moment! Were you to see as We do the Magnificent Light in many Life Streams of the Younger Generation, and all of that delayed or shut off because they drive them to drink and depravity in a few years—O Dear Ones, it's tragic beyond expression! And I am determined, just as determined, to dissolve that stuff from the Universe that has so depraved mankind, as I was to remove the black magicians! And thanks to you, it has been done! *(applause)* Thank you, Precious Ones.

And while you are standing, may I ask you to send forth your Call, and demand that the Cosmic Christ Legions of Cosmic Blue Flame sweep into the lower atmosphere of Earth and take Their Cosmic Toll in the beast of the world! Use those Words! And when I speak of that beast, it is not only the war beast, but it's all its claws! But if you ask for those Cosmic Christ Legions of Cosmic Blue Flame to sweep everywhere in the lower physical atmosphere of Earth, and take their Cosmic Toll in the beast of the world! The liquor and dope beast and other channels shall die as they should! *(applause)* Thank you, Precious Ones.

I want to reveal to you that the third one who went to the Great Central Sun with the Beloved Goddess of Liberty and Myself was **the Great Cosmic Angel on whose Crown blazes the Word "Union"!** *(applause)* Beloved Ones, I'm revealing to you tonight certain Inner Actions of the Law concerning your Nation. **The Goddess of Liberty and the Cosmic Angel with Myself have taken the Responsibility of removing the liquor beast and those destructive cravings from the emotional bodies of this Nation, and that's not a light task!** *(applause)* Thank you, Beloved Ones.

When you realize the creations in the emotional bodies of the people who are caught in that beast's destructive activity—the beast of war and all its claws—those creations are frightful to behold! But I tell you that when the Legions, the Cosmic Christ Legions of Cosmic Christ Blue Flame approach those beasts, their terror is worse—and they are to face that by My Command! *(applause)* Thank you. Their torture, their depravity, and their destruction has been frightful and inexcusable, and they must be annihilated from the Universe. And I shall appreciate, as well as the Beloved Goddess of Justice, and this Mighty Cosmic Angel who came to Washington—We shall appreciate every ounce of energy you give, every Call you make, until that condition is removed from the Universe, and its record blasted from Life. It must be done! There is no hope for mankind's Freedom until those frightful things are withdrawn and placed in the Violet-blue Flame where they cannot exist longer.

Therefore My Gratitude to you is boundless. And may I say to you, the hour when those things are removed, and the mankind of Earth feels the release from those frightful torturing cravings, will your gratitude and your love know what it means to stand to the Light and carry It high—until those in the darkness are drawn back Home into the Heart of that which is Eternal Happiness. And when you see those Life Streams one by one coming back to the condition in which is their Divine Birthright, you will know as We do that it's worth every effort you would ever make to compel those forces into annihilation. And you will be grateful with all you are

and have for the way and means that the Mighty
Saint Germain has given you by which you could
force the beast to take its claws off of Life and
to compel its annihilation.

Then will you know the Secret and the Power
of Mastery! Then will you feel it is worth every
effort you ever made to compel that thing to
cease its torture of God's Life. Great has been
mankind's defiance of the Requirements of the
Cosmic Law, but Great shall be your Joy and
Mine when by God's Almighty Cosmic Light so
dazzling they dare not look into It—when It comes
and becomes the atmosphere of Earth, entering
into all, and you see those forces cease to exist—
will you know what Gratitude to your "I AM
Presence" and to the Mighty Saint Germain and
the Ascended Host means. When you see your
loved ones arise in the God Light and Beauty and
Perfection of that "I AM Presence" and go forward in constructive, beautiful accomplishment,
your Hearts will know a gratitude that nothing
else could ever explain! Won't you be seated,
please.

Now I must not keep you longer tonight, but
I just wanted you to have the encouragement and
the Gratitude of Our Hearts for opening the

Door by which We may use more Light to dissolve these frightful things that have caused such distress to Life. May I say to you when these things are removed, will you also see disease and insanity removed, with them. So while the task is great, the Reward is greater. The Happiness that will be yours is Immortal—and that is well worth every effort you make to set Life Free! You are this far in the Light. Now with the Powers that are yours and your Calls to Us, you may draw others, and others and others to this same place, where they, too, will turn and join Us in the Great Work of cleansing the Earth. The Legions of Light and Love and Wisdom and Power are your Friends to the end of that Accomplishment!

May you feel the Power of that Cosmic Light; and may the Mighty Angel on whose Crown blazes the Word "Union," in that Authority of Cosmic Light which is His—and He whose Task it is to issue that Fiat—may He come quickly, visible to all, and issue the Command for that intensity of the Cosmic Light that shuts off war from the Earth forever! *(applause)* Beloved Ones, remember Her Words to Washington, the Being who came to Him, [Goddess of Liberty] and remember the Words of the Great Cosmic Angel on whose Crown blazoned the Word "Union," when He placed the Standard and said, "SO LONG AS THE STARS REMAIN AND THE HEAVENS SEND DOWN DEW, SO LONG SHALL THE UNION LAST!" And the people kneeling down, will say "I AM," and will give that "Mighty Presence" the credit that is their Freedom! Unto that Care of that "Mighty Presence" do I commend you tonight! He, the Cosmic Angel on Whose Crown blazes the Word Union and to She, the one who gave Washington the Vision—may Their Outpouring to your Nation tonight move into outer Action the Manifestations to which all bow, including Us; for when that Light comes, We all are Grateful with Love that is Immortal. May It become your Mantle of Protection, your Scepter of Power, your Pathway to Freedom, and your Immortal Victory without limit, and Its Cosmic Authority ever yours to use with full Power. Thank you and good night. Won't you be seated, please.

CHAPTER II

BELOVED ARCHANGEL MICHAEL

Chicago, Illinois
April 22, 1950
Record CD 1408

My Beloved Legions of Blue Flame, thank you for your fiery spirit tonight! Thank you for your faithfulness. Thank you for your willingness to stand with Us and drive through the jungle of human creation and blaze the Blue Flame that all will understand! Thank you for your Presence tonight as I have never thanked you before! With all the Power at Our Command are We watching every opportunity. We shall draw into the lower atmosphere of Earth everything the Cosmic Law will permit to prevent the holocaust intended. Stand your ground!

Yield no power to the human, and with all your breathing being, know that no weapon prospers against you. Don't forget that Decree! No weapon prospers against your America regardless of appearances. The sinister force can change its appearance from moment to moment, but We are changeless Authority, Immortal Power, and Ever-expanding Perfection! We are the Protecting Power of Life, and the sinister force, under the guise of protection, when it sends a nation to war, gloats over those who are its victims. The reckoning of the ages is here, and the destructive forces must cease their existence. Regardless of appearances, yield not an inch! Charge yourselves with Our Immortal Power! Feel your Immortal Authority to command the annihilation of that which dishonors God, and you shall have Legions come to your assistance that the rest of mankind do not even know exist.

Do you know, Beloved Ones, you who have loved the Beings of the Elements, you who bless and pour your love to the Powers of Nature, you do not realize what Friends you have in the Beings of the Elements. You do not quite understand how the Powers of Nature could protect you. But I do! They are My obedient Servants, and I shall command them to give their Blessing to you! *(long applause)* Thank you, Precious Ones, with all My Heart's Love. Won't you be seated, please.

Tonight I want to remind you of one intense action which you can easily draw forth into outer physical manifestation in the calling forth of the Immortal Power of the Angels of Blue Flame. Now don't hesitate, and don't forget this. Please call this forth sometime each day around everybody and everything under this Radiation. That is a certain Group of the Angelic Host which comes under My Direction. It's one of the Groups. When you call forth the Immortal Power of the Angels of Blue Flame, there isn't anything can use that Power but Perfection. You do not need to fear It. It doesn't contain anything for you but Immortal Protection and Immortal Perfection—but It contains an Action of Power that the sinister force knows better than to approach. I offer you this tonight that you may build a momentum of It around those you hold near and dear, and around all under this Radiation by daily Command.

Draw forth, command and demand the outer physical manifestation of the Immortal Power of the Angels of Blue Flame. You will know what Ascended Master Friends means! The sinister force cannot call those Beings. The sinister force could not be protected by Them, but Their Love for you would auto-

matically flow within Their Blue Flame. They
would love to protect you, because it is My Desire! We have specialized, recently, on one quality
or one special activity after another, any one of
which, if held to, will take you through to your
Immortal Victory. And We are releasing at this
time terrific dynamic Force and Action of the
Fire Element in the various channels to which
all of you are attuned. One may feel one action
of the Law more Powerful for your individual
needs, and another one feel something else. Accept that to which you feel the greatest attraction,
and then use It in outer Command by great
Happiness—with great delight! What in the world
have you to fear by reaching up and simply
embracing the Great God Power of Immortality?
What could come to you but Perfection? What
could you experience but Happiness? What
could you know but Its Truth?

Now when you call It in and around your-
selves, then will you become acquainted with Its
Glorious Blessing. So do not be afraid to use My
Immortal Power of the Angels of Blue Flame.
That is an Action of Love that contains within
It whatever might be required on the moment
under any set of circumstances to keep you con-

nected with Our Octave; and through that connection there would flow to you—on the instant, before any destruction could act—there could flow any unusual Power from Our Octave to protect you. We want this to be brought into an outer momentum which you may see sometimes, but at all times you would feel.

Demand the annihilation of all doubt and fear! Just accept Us and accept that We do love you! Accept that We are real! Experiment with Our Calls! Visualize their fulfillment, and Reality must appear for you! Then you can go forward, and by your own Conscious Command such as you've given tonight, cause the removal from the Earth of things that have tortured you for centuries—and tortured the mass of mankind. You have to have Power to do that, My Dear Ones because the sinister force is heavily energized. But when you call forth Our Immortal Power, it means that whatever amount of Power you call forth at any one time, that becomes anchored there for all Eternity. That becomes active for you in that capacity. Wherever you move, that is around you. It is a Divine Gift, indescribable in words. Only as you see Its Tremendous Action, only as you know Its Cosmic Power, only as you experiment with what It can do for you, will you have some glimpse into the Heights of Our Attainment and into the Realms of the Power-house of God.

Charge yourselves with Our Immortal Power and with the Immortal Love of the Angels of Blue Flame. I am charging you tonight to replace the energy you have sent forth, and that is your Gift for Eternity. Demand the Immortal Power of Our Love! It can fill you with Its Strength and Energy. It can expand through you Its various Powers of Action, because It contains Powers as well as Power. On the instant, if you get the feeling of this, you would be able to do many things that you have never done before in the way of Transcendent Activities, because Love—being the Great Treasure House of the Mighty Gifts of Life from the "Mighty I AM Presence" in the Great Central Sun—that Love can release to you at any moment the capacity and the way and means of doing things that produce greater Perfection for you. But they would be perfectly natural because they would be within your own Life.

Resistance, My Dear Ones, due to human discord in the physical octave, can be crashed easily.

That which you must call forth—the Light of your own Life to pass through in the great natural Law of the unfoldment of your Life—that is another thing. The Light just penetrates that and takes you through happily. This word "crash" that you were using tonight has a certain Power of its own. Everyone receives a certain feeling when you use that word, because it does carry within it a certain action with which the human, or the outer intellectual consciousness, is quite familiar. You know, when one is very determined, you use the expression, "Well, he crashed the gates!" That means you broke through the barriers. When a thing crashes it breaks into pieces, doesn't it? Well then, it's been demolished so far as its action is concerned. You have shut off its action. Please hold this picture through these Decrees tonight, that that Power may go forth into certain channels and act in its most needed way! Aren't you feeling stronger already? *(applause)*

Precious Ones, while you are standing, just a moment, feel yourselves like a Cup receiving this Outpouring—to give you ten times more than you have sent forth tonight. *(silence)* Isn't it amazing what the atomic structure will do? Isn't it amazing what changes can take place in a few

moments? You've had the experience tonight!
One moment you are in those intense Decrees—
the next moment you are at Peace. Isn't that
wonderful? The outer world can't do that for
you! Won't you be seated, please. Thank you.

*Now take time, Precious Ones, in your daily activi-
ties, take time to go somewhere alone for five minutes
and just still that outer, and then turn and call our
Immortal Power of the Angels of Blue Flame whose
Love is indescribable and can heal and can control
anything.* They have never been human, the majority of Them at least. They are Special Beings
created to intensify that Love in the Blue Flame
and focus It to give Its Boundless Blessings wherever They are loved and drawn into outer Action
by Conscious Command. They live to do the
Will of Love. Therefore you who call Them forth
into outer action by the Immortal Power of My
Love and Authority, you are very welcome, very
welcome to Their Special Activities tonight! You
might call Them My, shall I say, "pet Angels,"
because I need Them and use them so much!
They are quite fond of doing My Will! So tonight
as I offer you this Reminder to use the Immortal Power of Their Love of the Blue Flame, you
shall have very delightful results. Don't be afraid

to use It! It can never do anything to you but that which makes you happy. And what It does to the sinister force is the sinister force's education! *(laughter)*

Poor, benighted individuals who say there is no God, when they leave those bodies this time will face that which will cure them of that attitude for all time to come! *(applause)* Precious Ones, thank you with all My Heart. But do you know, Beloved Ones tonight, the Earth has been through this same thing time and time and time and again. This time, thanks to your Beloved Saint Germain and the Strength of that Blessed Godfre—*(applause)* thank you, Precious Ones. Thanks to the strength of Our Beloved Godfre, *(applause)* and to the Love of the Mighty Beloved Sanat Kumara, the end of that thing has to come upon the Earth now. *(applause)* Thank you, Precious Ones. While for some it might be strenuous for a time, yet the Powers of Nature will sigh with relief when that is finished!

May this night bless you with the Power of My Love Immortal, the Immortal Power of that Blue Flame of such Love as only Those who have become Its Presence can ever know, and whose Happiness is yours for Eternity. It is My Immortal Gift to you all, Precious

Ones. And because of the mighty Service you've rendered, I bear the Gratitude of the Ascended Host to you all. May you go on as the Victors of the Immortal Love whose Cosmic Authority and Immortal Power comes now upon the Earth to take Its Dominion, this time in Full Cosmic Action! *(applause)* My Precious Ones, thank you tonight with all My Heart forever. Won't you be seated, please.

Now I must not keep you longer. Thank you for your gift! Thank you for your strength, your courage, and your willingness to send forth this Power. We shall qualify It with everything that the Cosmic Law will permit, and may Its Immortal Expanding Action become visible to mankind and illumine them in ways they will never forget! With that which is approaching in the Release of the Cosmic Light, may Wave after Wave of Its Presence flow in, through and around you, and out over your Nation, and then out over the world. May those Waves of Cosmic Light come fast enough to offset and prevent that which otherwise would again take its toll. We are hoping for certain Assistance from the Cosmic Law, and when it is gained We shall not move—or lose one action in one *instant's* time—

in bringing into outer action that which takes the sinister force where it is to be forever consumed! *(applause)*

Thank you, Precious Ones. And tomorrow, if you would, give a Decree for the "Mighty I AM Presence" to come through all Life on the Earth and crash all desire to oppose God, the "Mighty I AM Presence," and the Perfection of Life's Divine Plan. It will help, quickly, to bring many into this Activity and to weed out from the sinister force those whom it has held under its hypnotic control. Won't you be seated, please.

Now in the Mantle of My Immortal Love and the Armor of Its Immortal Power, may I clothe you tonight. May the Great Blazing Presence from the Great Central Sun reveal Its Shining Face to you, and on the Ray of Love from Its Heart may you feel by Conscious Command— any moment that you stop and give It your attention—may you feel Its Response and the Limitless Supply of Our Energy, and all else, flow to you by the Love of the Angels of Blue Flame. May My Heart prove to you My Gratitude through the Action of this which I offer you tonight. Thank you. May you accept It; and may It bring you Immortal Joy, Immortal Indepen-

dence of every limitation—Immortal Freedom!
May that Love abide with you in Eternal Command. Thank you.

ARCHANGEL MICHAEL

CHAPTER III

BELOVED ELOHIM OF PEACE

Los Angeles, California
September 27, 1950
Cassette 65067

Beloved Ones of the Light, I trust I may adopt you and call you My "Legions of Peace"! That's quite an honor you know, and if you can live up to it, it will be a most wonderful experience for you. I shall show you now what that means in the outer world, because I'm going to ask you that wherever there seems to be turmoil or mistakes or problems, demand a Flame of My Victorious Peace to come forth where the discord seems to be, and be established there for Eternity. Now if you will call these Flames into outer physical action—I mean into the physical octave—to act in physical conditions under your authority, and ask Them to be made Eternal, there are certain of the Legions of the Sacred

29

Fire who are ready at hand and are awaiting the opportunity to bring as much of this Activity of the Sacred Fire into the lower physical octave as soon as possible.

This is a stabilizing, powerful Action, and much of it comes under the Guardianship of the Seraphim. I want you to feel deeply tonight your intense love to the Seraphim of Peace; for They are the Guardians of these Flames which We are hoping through your Calls to, as you might say, "plant" permanently into the physical octave wherever you call Them forth. Unless something of this sort is done, Precious Ones, where We can draw a very great Power of the Sacred Fire into the outer physical octave; unless there is an intensity of that Flame drawn into the physical world, the constant surging of discord is such a continual disturbance, that where individuals do maintain a certain amount of harmony, it is not left undisturbed long enough to let it become a permanent action in the locality where you desire it to be. And it is to bring a greater Guard around all of you that We are offering this tonight.

The Legions of the Seraphim who guard these very intense Activities of the Sacred Fire are awaiting every channel of service that it is pos-

sible to give at this time. But since mankind
know so little about Them, and most people
doubt of Their very existence, they do not have
very much opportunity to draw into the physical
octave these greater Activities of the Sacred Fire
that otherwise could come and be a greater Consuming Power to discordant conditions. But if
you will accept Them as real, you will find Their
Blessing is real. If you demand these Flames be
made Eternal where you call Them forth, when
the intensity of that Power reaches a certain
point, They will be permanently established.

The Great Cosmic Law is using every conceiv-
able opportunity to draw into the physical world
as much as possible these more Magnificent Powers from the Great Realms of the Sacred Fire, in
order to help those who seek the constructive
way of life to be strong enough and to stand
against that which seeks to engulf them. But since
"I AM" Peace to the Earth and it is My, not only
prerogative, but My Responsibility at a certain
point to establish this Flame throughout a certain
proportion of the Earth in order to make Peace
permanent to the world; therefore I shall appreciate greatly every Call you make to have—now
mark My Words—the Immortal Flame of My

Victorious Peace take the place of everything that comes to your attention that is disturbing. Wherever you can stop long enough to make the Call silently and demand this Flame come forth, We shall see that It does come forth! But the Demand must be made in the physical octave, and then the Flame does the rest. And since those of you who have made some Calls to the Great Cosmic Christ Legions of the Guarding Seraphim, it is in Answer to that Call that We hope to accomplish much through this Acknowledgment and this Decree.

Please acknowledge, Precious Ones, in everything you do, acknowledge the Victory you want, because that Acknowledgment is in reality the manifestation of what you desire; and when that becomes deeply enough set as a habit, it will bring almost instantaneous outpicturing in the physical octave. If you want Peace to become permanent, then you must DEMAND THE VICTORY OF THE PEACE OF ETERNITY! I'm saying this with force tonight because the Peace mankind have had from time to time came from Our Great Love and Our Great Realm of Life. But It was not qualified as Eternal; It was not acknowledged as Victorious over all in this world.

Hence It came, and when mankind felt discordant, they rebelled against It and drove It away. But when you begin your Demand for the Flame of the Victorious Peace of Eternity descend into a condition where the human seems to be and take Its Dominion there with Full Power; then it will be almost like drawing individual Suns of Flame here and there into the substance that has been qualified with darkness.

But do acknowledge It as *the Victorious Peace of Eternity, the Flame of Victorious Peace of Eternity*. And if within yourselves sometimes there seems strain or stress that is disturbing, and you'll stop for just a moment and you give that Acknowledgment, "I AM" the Law of the Victorious Peace of Eternity—you will find scarcely before you get through saying the Words, the rate of vibration which that is in the Universe has released through you—and you will begin to feel quiet. You will feel things stilling, and the clearness coming that will enable you to have the harmony to think clearly, to see ahead, and to know unmistakably the Divine Plan; and then to be for you the Strength in yourselves to fulfill that Plan.

You see, through the centuries, My Loved Ones, people have wanted to fulfill the Divine

Plan, and they have wanted to very sincerely. And then when the opportunity was offered, they were not strong enough to do it. It's like a little child wanting to be an athlete before it grows up. But now, with these Calls and your Acknowledgement of the Victory which you want here, then when you acknowledge that you are the Law; then the Law acts in you with whatever Power is necessary to produce that Victory. If you begin to acknowledge, "'I AM' the Law of the Victorious Christ which I desire manifest here in outer physical action"; then Dear Hearts, if you were not quite as strong as you should be to produce that manifestation, the strength would come into you in order to produce the Fulfillment of your Acknowledgment of the Law's Authority in the physical octave.

When you acknowledge the Law of the Victorious Christ, well then, Precious Ones, your own energy has gone forth vibrating with that Call and that desire. And since you are acknowledging, when you say the "Victorious Christ," the Fulfillment of the Divine Plan of your own Higher Mental Body, it would automatically pour into you the strength or whatever was necessary to fulfill Its own Divine Plan—when you begin to demand that It is Victorious here through you. Now this will be of tremendous benefit in healing, Precious Ones. You can give tremendous Healing and Peace by this Call. If your loved ones are in distress, and you wish to give that assistance to Life; and you demand the Flame of Victorious Peace of Eternity to enter into the flesh structure and become the Purity, the Strength, the Love, and the Power to correct a condition, it will be so.

We want you have this Freedom, and as you live closer in your Calls to the Guarding Seraphim, you will find very Great Love filling your worlds as if by magic, in a perfectly natural way with those things you desire—I mean when they are the desires that fulfill the Ascended Masters' Divine Plan. Oh! if people who are prodded and tortured by their human desires would only demand the Satisfaction and the Contentment of the Victorious "Mighty I AM Presence" in themselves, they wouldn't have any struggle, Precious Ones. The "Presence" doesn't struggle when It manifests Its Victory. It pours Its Love out and breathes into outer manifestation the form you desire. But people are tortured by their own desires and those in the atmosphere about them because they have not called forth the satisfaction and the contentment of their own Victory. And you can't have contentment Precious Ones, you can't have satisfaction unless you do have the Victory of your "Presence," because anything that might seem to be so from the outer standpoint, unless it is the Perfection of your "Presence," would only be a temporary thing; and as soon as it's gone, your satisfaction and contentment would be gone too.

So when I call into outer action Our Victorious Peace of Eternity, you have scarcely to think of that until on the chest will you begin to feel a soft tingling sensation as the Flame begins Its Expansion and Its Radiation into the atmosphere about you; for this has to take place through the expansion of the Flame in your own Heart. So when you acknowledge that that is the Law of the Victorious Peace of Eternity, My Dear Ones, if you'll let that be the Law in your world, there won't be anything but the Peace which allows you to fulfill the Divine Plan and sustains Its Blessings in your world until Peace is yours for Eternity.

People in their Hearts rebel, or in their feeling world, rebel against discord and disturbance and mistakes and problems, and they fight, fight, fight them. But they don't call the Victory of the opposite thing into themselves and into the problems to become that which will keep them satisfied and contented. I assure you, Precious Ones, the human desires are a ceaseless craving. They are the bottomless pit, and you can never satisfy them. You crave this, that, and the other thing, and as soon as you get it, you crave something else. But that's not true from your own "Beloved I AM Presence" standpoint! When you crave your "Presence" and you demand Its Victorious Presence inside of you, and you demand the Flame of Its Victorious Peace of all Eternity; well then, there comes the satisfaction in doing anything you want to do that brings you permanent Happiness. You will find all that restlessness, that discontent and depression and uncertainty and doubt and fear will have been gone—as if they had never existed.

I'm sure you feel this in the atmosphere tonight; and were you to see the building, I'm sure you would be delighted. It is enclosed in a Sun of My Heart's Love that I assure you is Eternal Peace. May you forever feel yourselves clothed in My Heart's Flame of Victorious Peace of Eternity;

for I assure you, nothing in all time to come could ever change the Peace of My Love! Therefore when you demand the Victorious Peace of Eternity, you have demanded that Love from your own "I AM Presence." Love from Our Octave has become in you the Law governing all the energy in and around you, with that feeling of contentment and satisfaction that becomes the permanent Outpouring of Perfection without limit from your own "I AM Presence"–from Our Octave. And It will become a Magnet to draw to you from the physical world whatever you require to give you the Assistance in fulfilling the Great Divine Plan as the Ascended Masters direct.

Then will you enter into the real Music of the Spheres. Then will you know as you enter that stillness that to enter that Peace brings with it a Light in which you may see all things clearly ahead, and know the direct, perfect, simple, harmonious way to do everything. Then your struggle ceases! Then your mistakes are no more, and then will your very Radiation be a Benediction to Life and fill the Universe with the Light that casts no shadow.

O Precious Ones, that in itself is a tremendous Decree! Were you to take the Statement, " 'I AM' the Law and Visible Manifestation of the Light that casts no shadow, the Light of Eternity in which I see all Perfection," you will bring to yourselves marvelous Blessings, a relaxation, a clearness of consciousness and absolute certainty of that which is ahead which you may select, bring into outer use, fulfill the Divine Plan, and then go on your way to expand still greater manifestations.

This is the way, Precious Ones, we fulfill those Great Words of the Master Jesus, "Behold I make all things new," by this Flame of Victorious Peace of Eternity. When My Flame comes in at that Command, the old dissolves and the new becomes permanently established in Its Ever-expanding Perfection. And this you must have, Dear Hearts, before you can bring certain things into outer use that belong to the new Cycle, that belong into outer physical action for those who will remain on the Earth in the next—in the whole incoming Cycle.

Now your own worlds, Precious Ones, can just as well become this Peace now if you will so decree it, as to still be the outpicturing of the result of mistakes in the past. If the mistakes of the past have produced discord in the present, well, you are all-authority to reach out and take that discord and transmute it by your Violet Consuming Flame which purifies it. And then as you acknowledge that: "*'I AM' the Flame of the Victorious Peace of Eternity that now becomes the Perfection of all I desire in outer physical action, and keeps the door locked for Eternity against any future mistakes.*" Then everything you do each day will build that Manifestation of the Divine Plan's Fulfillment and becomes Eternal in Its Great Blessing to you and through you to the world.

Oh! when the world is seething with war, My Dear Ones, this Command is very paramount in Its Blessing to those who will give It. You might stand amidst the wreck of worlds, and if you gave this Command, you would be held at Peace. I use that expression, but there is no such thing as a wreck of worlds. That's an expression you use in the outer life. You might stand amidst the wreck of physical things, but you would stand untouched by them so long as you give this Acknowledgment. And it is to the degree that you demand this into outer action that We can be of greater Assistance to you by sending those of the Angelic Host who will bring as intense an action from time to time as the condition in hand requires.

O Precious Ones, if you'll begin to acknowledge this inside of your bodies, you will feel such
rest! Those blessed atomic structures that you
abide in, they will bless you forever if you will
give this Command; for it will be such a relief to
the outer senses of your feeling world that you
will feel as if tons of pressure had been taken off
of you and your world. You can just as well demand that your world be now a Complete Flame
of the Victorious Peace of Eternity; and you live
and move and have your being in the Heart of
Its Love—contented, satisfied, at Peace for Eternity—yet ever active in the greater creation of
more and more Perfection that expands at your
Command, is sustained to bless all, and ever goes
forward to fulfill the Great Divine Plan.

When the Great Beings of the Angelic Host
offer the Blessing of Their Love to hold those
Flames in a condition until the condition is dis-
solved, Great is the Joy, My Dear Ones, when
They can come close enough to Earth to compel
that change to take place at your own Conscious
Command. They are Beings of Love, and Their
Service is to Love alone. Therefore, when through
Love you call forth for Their Presence to come
and help establish this in the outer physical

octave, that It may become the Eternal Peace of the Ascended Masters' Great World—Their Great Realm of Activity—well, the Great Beings who have waited to accomplish this for so long send the Angelic Host. And Their Joy is boundless the moment They begin to accomplish this which has to be done in the outer in order to anchor certain Power that is constructive in the physical world, to hold the Earth itself from shattering to pieces.

So your Call is vitally important, quite as well for your Nation and the world as it 'tis for your own individual affairs. Send your Love to the Beloved Seraphim and see for yourselves the Love that comes back to you. Make your Calls to the Angelic Host for Their Victorious Love to come into the outer physical manifestation that holds Command for Eternity. Call Their Love here, as well as pouring your own love into a condition, and see for yourselves what Their Service is! See what Their Power of Love can produce! See how real, how practical, how sensible, and how powerful is the Love that They can direct, and the Love that should be everywhere in the world.

Someone—sometime, somewhere—must draw that Love and fill the world with that Activity of the Sacred Fire if you are ever to be free from these other conditions. The Angelic Host are the Messengers from the Great Central Sun, the Beings provided to draw those Flames into the physical world until the world itself has become a Sun of Everlasting Love. When you demand the Victorious Love of the Angelic Host become the Law and the Authority of your outer action, it will be so! And if you acknowledge, " 'I AM' the Law of the Victorious Love of the Great Angelic Host in outer physical action in all I do," you will find strain and struggle gone. You will find Perfection appearing, and Joy will be yours that none can change. It is well worth your most sincere trial in everything you do in the outer life. After all, when hate has darkened your planet and has robbed you of the Peace that God gave you in the beginning, then if you call again for the Love that is the natural condition of this world—the Love that belongs here, the Love that was here in the beginning, the Love that ought to be here now, the Love that must come and hold Command in the future—if you will call the Victory of the Love of the Angelic Host here, more people will begin to feel and accept the reality of the Angels. More will begin to feel that

They are real Beings who render a Service and answer the Calls of those who serve the constructive way of life.

These must be called into outer action! My Dear Ones, mankind have driven away the Great Beings who blessed them for centuries. Those Beings had to recede because mankind deliberately said they didn't want Them. Now then, if conditions are to be permanently improved, then mankind must call and ask for Their return instead of denying Their very existence. So when you, the Beloved of the Light, make your Calls to the Seraphim, and you demand and acknowledge the Law of the Victorious Love of the Angelic Host to act now and forbid the existence of hate, you will render tremendous service to your Nation, to yourselves, and to the world. And hate, you will find one day, rolled back like a scroll; and the dark clouds drawn into the compound till that substance is purified in the Blue Flame and the Violet Flame, and returned to the great universal use of Life.

That substance of hate must recede; and therefore when you acknowledge the Law of the Victorious Love of the Angelic Host and the Victorious Peace of Eternity, you are calling ac-

tual Light into the physical octave. And then as
those Powers of the Sacred Fire and the actual
Flames themselves become anchored in and
around you, and wherever you call Them forth,
you will find the Light increasing that brings the
Ascended Masters' Consciousness to the mankind of Earth; and they will become intelligent
and obedient and purified and harmonized to the
point where they will cooperate with the Great
Cosmic Law that seeks to set them Free.

So in the Arms of that Great Flame may I ask
you to feel yourselves held. Great Flames from
Our Mighty Realm of Activity, the Sevenfold
Flame of the Victorious Peace of Eternity, is yours
to demand—abide in the physical world wherever
you command It to come forth. And if you will
take your Authority and acknowledge yourselves
as the Law of Its Manifestation in outer physical
action, it will come to pass, and I hope quickly.
So as My Heart is ready and willing to give you
more of the Activity of the Fire Element and be
the Victorious Peace of Eternity—which is Love's
Light to the Earth that annihilates all darkness. I
shall deeply appreciate every Call that you can
send forth as soon as possible. I trust I shall make
Myself very tangibly felt in the Blessings that I

will pour back through My Love and Gratitude to you, to once again help mankind give Acknowledgment to the Reality of the Angelic Host.

There is the Flame of My Peace in each forehead radiating through the atomic structure of the brain, so part of My own Life Flame is in each of you. Therefore, when you say, " 'I AM' the Law of the Victorious Peace of Eternity," you are speaking an Eternal Truth; for that very Flame is already abiding in you, and through that, you become the Law of the Peace which "I AM." When you call the Great Presence of the Guarding Seraphim to blaze Their Flame of Their Love wherever you want this Peace made manifest permanently, then Their Love brings more Life. And where Their Love is, hate can never come. Where My Peace is acknowledged as the Law, discord can never again approach. So I give you a Sanctuary, a Place of Safety from the discord of the outer world; and if you care to withdraw into the Great Altar of Its Presence, you will find there the Power of Perfection's Flame, the Happiness and Contentment and Satisfaction of Eternity, and the Boundless Blessings you have always known somewhere ought to be in outer action.

Now the Door is open! Now is the opportunity to give obedience to this Law and make this Call, and let Us see how quickly that may become the Great Fulfillment of the Divine Law that releases the Dispensation; and the Cosmic Fiat goes forth that compels hate to leave the Earth forever. Great is your opportunity! Great is your responsibility! Great is your privilege to serve Life, and once again make the Law of Its Love the Authority of this Octave, and you yourselves, the Flame of Its Eternal Victory of Love and Peace and Power and Perfection that is boundless. I wrap you in Its Everlasting Love. May Its Blessings forever go forth, expanding through you to reach all mankind until the Light claims Its own, and intensifies until there are no more shadows, and not even a memory of anything but the Eternal Joy of expanding Perfection and Peace and Love through Eternity.

Thank you, and I make My Flame expand within you and clothe you in Its outer Presence until you feel It and others feel It. And then let Its Light become the Visible Radiation that will make mankind know the Truth and the Reality of the Angelic Host and Ourselves, that the Door may be wide open for Their greater Freedom for

Life—for all Life on this Earth. Your Freedom to Life brings greater Freedom to you. Our Peace to you brings greater Love and Peace from the Central Sun to Us, and the system will grow brighter because of your Love and your desire for the Victorious Peace of Eternity. May Its Beauty fill your world, Its Music ever be the Eternal Harmony and Blessing of all in and around you; and Victory wherever you move establish Its Love and Peace of Eternity. I thank you.

CHAPTER IV

BELOVED GODFRE

Shasta Springs, California
October 21, 1951
Record CD 1279

Dear Hearts of the Light, in just a few Words, I want to add My Love and Blessing and Gratitude to you all for all that has been accomplished during this Conclave, and all that is yet to be done through that which you will carry back with you to expand Its Service among whom you move. Great has been the accomplishment here, and may you go on each day strengthened beyond your fondest dreams in your use of this Cosmic Christ Fire; and know that It is the most imperative thing required in your Nation tonight—Our Nation—God's Nation!

Only that Sacred Fire whose Love throughout Creation is the Law of Life's Perfection can be brought into outer conditions! Only that Love and that Sacred Fire can remove those things that seek to torture you and the loved ones within the Land. Tonight, charge forth and see the United States of America a Blazing Immortal Victory of this Cosmic Christ Fire! See the atmosphere over the Nation blazing that Violet Consuming Flame with such Pressure that It holds absolutely motionless everything that is destructive, and enables the constructive activities and individuals to go forward into conditions and hold the balance of all that is required to shut off that which seeks to destroy you.

Great has been the Outpouring day after day since the first of last January! And We must continue It; and the more you can remember to call forth the Immortal Victory of this Cosmic Christ Fire that consumes everything that distresses you, will you feel your Greater Freedom hourly almost from that which heretofore has been your struggle. If problems appear, distress seems to approach, keep calling this into outer action, and demand that your world from tonight is the Immortal Victory of such Cosmic Christ Fire as shall hold the Christ Victorious over everything on this Earth, because it must be so!

Take your stand and demand Immortal Victory of the Cosmic Christ to blaze Its Cosmic Fire and consume, consume, consume forever, all that has cast a shadow upon Life! And We shall be with you! We shall be back of you! We shall go before you with this Flame, and do everything possible as you give Us a certain amount of your energy through these Calls. If you'll give Us a third of the energy, We will supply the other two-thirds. And may I say that as you demand the Immortal Victory of the Fiery Love of the Cosmic Christ, it will be easier to overcome the world's hate—as you demand this Fire in and around you and going before you to remove that which is the limitation that heretofore you have accepted.

The Law of Cosmic Christ Love must be the Law of the Earth! And It has to become the Law of you and your manifestations before the people in the outer world will use It enough to set themselves Free. Just know from tonight that you go forth the Cosmic Law of Cosmic Christ Fire. And the Cosmic Law's Demand for Its Love to be the Law of Control, wherever you go, moves into outer conditions these Activities of the Sacred Fire that move forward and simply take possession and hold Command.

We will be with you and strengthen everything within you to help you pour forth the Love and the Kindness that will hold the Protection about you. And the more you pour It forth, the less will you feel exhaustion or distress or strain in the body. There is nothing brings such relaxation, as the Immortal Victory of Cosmic Christ Fiery Love that is in Command of all physical action! So go forward with Happy Hearts, knowing you are held within the Immortal Protection of this Cosmic Christ Fire whenever you call It forth. *Know and call It forth with every ounce of your strength in everything you do! Just flash It forth, and then go on your way! Flash It forth again, and just demand that Its Immortal Victory come now into you and your conditions!* Its Immortal Victory, which is Immortal Love, protects and controls your loved ones. Its Immortal Victory, which is Immortal Power, charges into you and around you until the very Radiation brings Strength to those who are trying to hold to the constructive way of life.

Demand the Government of Cosmic Christ Fire, and Its Immortal Victorious Freedom giving the people the Love that sets them Free! The Land must be governed by that Love of the Sacred Fire which is the Directing Intelligence and Purity that holds Balance until all can make conscious effort toward the constructive way of life! My Dear Ones, don't hesitate to keep calling forth the Cosmic Angels of Cosmic Christ Fire! There are Limitless Legions of the Angelic Host who could come to your Assistance again and again as you draw this forth. And I know that you are already feeling the closer approach of the Angelic Host in your daily recognition and acceptance of Their Presence. Just demand the Visible, Tangible Presence of the Angelic Host who draw the Cosmic Christ Fire of Eternal Love into the physical octave, and blaze those Manifestations that compel mankind to see Them!

There is a certain acceptance in the mass feeling of mankind of Angels. They do not admit it too much, but all Life knows within itself there are such Beings. Therefore as you call forth the Angels of Cosmic Christ Fire, the Angels of Cosmic Christ Love, the Angels of Cosmic Christ Victory to be with you always in all outer physical conditions, you will find your Decrees answered very much more quickly; for when you demand this Love, Love answers on the instant! And know always that My Cosmic Heart is the Fire of that Love which I want to give you to set you Free! If you make the Call, I will give It, and when you receive It, you will find It does set you Free.

I just wanted to offer this, that It might enfold you as you return home to your destination, and make you feel that wherever We go, We are never apart—not an instant! That Love holds Command in, through, and around Us all; and We pour It forth, wherever there is the slightest opportunity offered. May It watch between thee and Me while We are absent one from another, and the Flame of Its Everlasting Victory bring you Its Choicest Blessings, and clothe you in Powers you know naught of until you begin to use Them in outer Action. And then you will know what Love has given and Love will yet bestow, until It is your World, your Pathway of Light, your physical action; and your Victory is assured wherever you abide. For the world is starving for this Love, and Life seeks It, and will receive It everywhere you pour It forth. Just go forward, and all that My Cosmic Heart can give shall attend you as a Living Flame to hold Command about you and bring you Blessings that I have long wanted to bestow.

Tonight may My Love unlock the Door to the Glories of Our Octave, and let Them flood to you all while you are yet unascended, that you may use Them in Greater Power while yet in your physical conditions, and thus assist others to turn to the Light—because the Magnet of that Love is coming stronger into the physical atmosphere of Earth to attract those who seek God and to serve God with Love that sets them Free.

In the Mantle of Its Everlasting Flame do I clothe you tonight. One day you will know all that I mean when I have called you "Dear Hearts of the Light"! I have held you in the Flame of My Cosmic Heart. May Its Love speak to you whenever you need Me, and give you the Blessings of all Eternity.

CHAPTER V

BELOVED
LADY MASTER NADA

Chicago, Illinois
January 8, 1952
Record CD 1283

Beloved of My Heart, We are very, very happy at the Inner Level when you are strong and powerful and courageous—and when you are fearless before the forces of this world. Therefore hesitate not to stand your ground against everything that has no right to live! Try to feel always that when there is anything that tries to deprave mankind or destroy that which God has given to lift mankind to greater Perfection, then know with every fiber of your being that those destructive creations of mankind have no right to live, because they are not given Authority of God to come into existence! Someday you must take your stand and have the Discrimination at the Inner Level to know whether a thing is the part of the Eternal Divine Plan or is not.

I want to take up the explanation of something tonight that I trust will clear your minds in many ways, because We have never entered very deeply into it; and yet it's time now that you understood for your own Protection. You have often heard Us speak of the Etheric Record of a thing. The Etheric Substance of your own outer self is the finest substance, so to speak, of the physical world, in the atomic structure of the body and of the mental and feeling body which each of you has. That Etheric Record, originally, before mankind created discord, held the Divine Pattern of the Perfection of Eternity for your entire Life Stream until your Ascension. That contained the Original Divine Plan of your activities through your journeys in the physical world through all your embodiments. But the etheric substance is, by its natural creation, able to take the record of discord, and those are the records that We have spoken of to be consumed—destructive records. It will retain the constructive ones, and that always produces Light within the body when the destructive records are com-

pletely consumed. Then the body itself begins to
radiate a Light that is visible and tangible to the
physical senses or the physical sight of life,
whether it be the life of a human being, or animal life in the outer world. All Life sees the Light
when the Etheric Body is purified.

Now when you hear Us, or sometimes others,
speak of the Akashic Records, that is a different
thing. The Akashic Records are of the Universe,
and They are recorded in the Eternal Light Substance that abides throughout Creation. They
hold the Eternal Divine Record of that which is
to be and *does not take* destructive records. That
is simply the location, so to speak, of the Divine
Plan of Creation, and contains for all time
ahead—aeons of time—that which is to be manifested in a system of worlds and in an individual
Life Stream, because that is the Pattern that is
also contained within the Heart Flame of your
Electronic Body and the Higher Mental Body of
your "Blessed I AM Presence." That is also contained within the permanent atom of your own
Heart. Now that will not take destructive records.

Sometimes people who do not understand the
difference between these two ways and means of
recording what has occurred in outer manifesta-

tion many times call the etheric record the
Akashic Record. But they are not the same, and
I want to make that clear tonight, so you will
not become confused when We begin to call
forth at a certain time the Akashic Records of
that which must come into being as the Incoming Civilization that is to become permanent in
this world—beginning first in the United States of
America.

Now then, the Akashic Record of each one's
own Life Stream—if you will keep the outer self
alert—will unfold within you from time to time
by the Command of the Higher Mental Body;
and you will just naturally build Its Perfection
out here, when the outer self is kept purified and
obedient to the Requirements of the "Mighty
I AM Presence." But let Me make this clear to
you: unascended beings, through certain attunement, can read, sometimes, the etheric record.
But they cannot read the Akashic Record. Only
an Ascended Being can read for centuries ahead
the Records of Life and that which is to be.

So don't let anybody claim to read the
Akashic Record. When they do, just know they
are not telling you the Truth—unless it be an Ascended Being. The only record that the outer self

can read or see is the etheric record. Sometimes it is constructive and sometimes it is not. And that's where the trouble comes. When people get mixed up in the psychic plane and begin to see things, because they see them doesn't mean that they are the Eternal Truth of Existence by any means! I want to give you this information to-night for your Protection. When people come and claim they can do those things, you have the Knowledge of the Truth of the Law, so don't believe them! If you want to fulfill the Akashic Record of your own Life Stream and outpicture Its Manifestation that brings Eternal Happiness and Perfection and Beauty to all the Universe, then call your "Beloved I AM Presence" to fulfill Its own Divine Plan through you and manifest the Ascended Masters' Perfection everywhere in this world. And just do that with great Devotion and Humility and Love and Purity to your "Presence," and don't brag about it!

This is a very Sacred Power. The purer and more obedient the outer self, the more the "Presence" will naturally fulfill Its own Divine Pattern through you in the outer; till the outer self becomes more like the Higher Mental Body until the two blend into one. If I were you, I would take the stand that your Higher Mental Body stand your guard, annihilate all destructive etheric records, and never let you see one! Then you will have certain Protection. But if you become curious about the etheric record of someone else, you'll certainly step into deep water from which you will not extricate yourself, because people do these things of their own Free Will. And if they open themselves to that attunement, even an Ascended Master will not close the door—because they do it of their own Free Will in deliberate defiance to the Knowledge and Truth of the Law that has been told mankind throughout all ages from the very beginning.

There is no time through the centuries in which mankind have not been told the Eternal Truth of the Law of the whole Universe, and the conditions that are manifesting today are created deliberately by defiance against that which was the Truth given in the beginning by which all manifestation could have been kept the Perfection of the Ascended Masters' Octave. The Perfection of the two first Golden Ages contained no discord or imperfection of any kind. Those two Golden Ages were the Perfection of Life that is coming down into manifestation. Now after the world is purified and cleansed, and mankind that are left here turn to God and are willing to give the Obedience, you will find, as the Golden Age proceeds, certain numbers of the Angelic Host who have never taken embodiment in the physical world on any planet will begin to take embodiment in the physical world to gain their experience life through the Harmony of that which is to become permanent to the Earth, and then attain their Ascension—Harmonious all the way through.

Now some of the Angelic Host are Ascended, and some are not. Some have been through the whole series of physical embodiments, and some have never come into physical embodiment. And since They know only the Service of the Love of the Sacred Fire, some have refused to come into embodiment until conditions are purified. Those who are Angel Devas and the Archangels have been through physical embodiments. Some of the Angels have, and some of Them have not. The Cherubim and Seraphim have not embodied in this world. They often come as Guardians of some Focus of the Sacred Fire, and They guard that with Their Love; but They are of very Great

Power and Purity whose Love alone is the only Quality that They have within Themselves, or that They can possibly manifest. They cannot manifest anything but the most Powerful Outpouring of the Sacred Love of the Sacred Fire.

These Blessed Beings are real. They are Eternal! They are provided by Life to guard the Manifestations of Beauty and Perfection that Love alone can create, that Love alone can sustain, and that Love alone can expand to ever Greater Perfection in Cosmic Manifestation. I want you to know something of this because the more you can recognize the Angelic Host, the more you can call Their Assistance to you, the more you can feel Their Closeness by the Love you send to Them, the closer They can come to you. And the closer They come into the outer atmosphere of Earth, the lower atmosphere, the more will the Radiation of Their Purity, Their Love, and Their Activity of the Sacred Fire hold Harmony and Protection around you. So They are of Powerful Assistance to help guard all constructive activities and give the Protection and Strength to those who are making the effort through this frightful time of outer chaos. When you are making the effort to hold to the God

Presence, the "Mighty I AM," these Great Beings,
if given recognition, are willing at all times to do
for mankind things they cannot do for themselves.

I've wanted you to understand this tonight,
because as you call more of the Angelic Host to
ever abide in and around each of you and your
loved ones, your homes, your Study Groups,
your Temples; Dear Ones, don't fail to call the
Angelic Host—all who can come to you—to fill
and surround your Temples and your Study
Groups and your Reading Rooms, and wherever this Magnificent Truth that the Mighty Saint
Germain and the Great Ones have given you is
held in Guard to render Its Service to mankind.

And when people, unfortunately, do not
value the Trust that Life has given them, it is
unfortunate indeed! It is an Honor, My Dear
Ones, to be given the Trust by Life, the "Mighty
I AM Presence," to guard a Focus of the
Ascended Masters' Activity, and to guard the
Gift They have given to be used in the Service
of the Light. It is an Honor; and I would like
everyone under this Radiation to understand that
each one, because of the Truth you have been
given and the Assistance that has come to you

from the Ascended Host in this Activity of the "I AM," each of you is a Guardian of the Gift that has been given to you, and through which you have received the Blessings that you have thus far.

So whether you are in a so-called position of authority or not does not mean that you're not a Guardian of this "I AM" Activity, to hold It Sacred and untouched by the depraved forces of the outer world. Each one who has been blessed by the Mighty Saint Germain through the Knowledge He has given is Honor-bound unto the Law of Life to be a Guardian of the Trust that Life has given—when It has poured forth the Truth of the Cosmic Law and the Radiation of Love and Purity and Power from the Ascended Masters by which the individual may attain His Ascension, and be the Channel to carry this Light to help others be Free in the Ascension also. So everyone who has the Knowledge and has been blessed by having the Love and Assistance of the Ascended Host is automatically expected to honor the Trust of knowing this Law and using Its Power in the physical octave to become Free.

So don't let anyone take the stand, "Well, I haven't been appointed, or I haven't been the one who is supposed to have the authority—somebody else has got the authority—I'm not, and so on!" Well, let Me tell you, everyone is entrusted by Life, the "Mighty I AM Presence" and the Ascended Host, with the Trust of guarding the divinest of things that Life can give in the Universe, and that's the Knowledge of the "Beloved I AM Presence"! *(applause)* Thank you, Beloved Ones. Won't you be seated, please.

Now why is this so? Because, My Dear Ones, it is an Honor to guard the Love that sets you Free. Surely people should understand that in the intellect, and automatically feel it and know it in the feeling body! So will each of you try to make that clear to others. And whether there is some particular position of authority or not matters not. Everyone who has received this Knowledge and has received the Blessings which It brings is Honor-bound unto the Law of Life to be the Guardian of It, to keep It pure and uncontaminated by mankind's concepts; and to use It to expand the Perfection and Purity of Life that lifts the rest of Life to Greater Purity and Freedom!

I want to make this clear, because greater Gifts will be given you, and the Law will expect you to guard Them. The Law will expect you to understand that a Trust by Life is an Honor to God. So if you will feel that, We can bring you many, many, many more Blessings by Powers that as yet you cannot quite draw into your outer direction. If the whole Student Body will understand this, and feel it their Sacred Duty to honor and protect the Knowledge that has come from the Mighty Saint Germain, and others of the Ascended Host and the Angelic Host called in and around you—and all your Group Activities, to guard Them against anything that is of dishonor or misunderstanding—then the Cosmic Law, if It sees that you are faithful in a few things, will make you Master over many! We are awaiting the opportunity to give you more hourly, that there may be more Power in the physical world to be the attraction to mankind that raises them into the greater Freedom of their own "Blessed I AM Presence."

These Great Beings that Life provides to ever guard Its Divine Gifts to mankind are real! They are provided by Life to guard the Great Gifts of Its own Expanding Consciousness and Perfection. Therefore those who receive Its Knowledge, automatically under the Cosmic Law become the Guardians of Its Expanding Perfection. And that

is an Honor—when Life trusts you with the opportunity to guard Its Divine Gifts to the Universe!
So if you will appreciate that, and then make it
clear to everyone under the Radiation that everybody is a Guardian of this Law to keep It pure,
clear, and uncontaminated by mankind's concepts! You don't have to have the Messenger say,
"Well, you're 'thus and so'—somebody else is
'thus and so.' " Life automatically gives you the
Divinest of Itself. And that is an Honor which
Life expects you to guard, that you may have a
Greater Gift. And then the Gift, as you give It to
someone else, if you keep It pure and protected,
will forever go on rendering Its Service to Life.
And Life will come back and bless you infinitely
everywhere you abide.

We want you to have both this Protection and
the Happiness and the Supply that Life is ever
willing to give and is surging—trying to give It
into the outer use of all who will use It construc-
tively. In this respect, as you hold closer to your
"Presence" and demand Its Love and Purity
guard everything that is God's Gift to Life, then
you will find unfolding to your outer consciousness—step by step—the next accomplishment that
your "Presence" wishes to manifest in the outer;

and each one will bring you greater Happiness than the one before. But after you manifest it, there must come the Power that protects it for future use of the rest of Life. And that is an Honor from Life Itself to the lesser Life, that it may forever carry forward the Blessings from above to the Universe around you for the Freedom and greater Happiness of Life everywhere.

So may the Flame of Love from My Heart be the Mantle of Protection about you all; for I, too, am Honor-bound to guard the Mighty Saint Germain's Work and Activity in the physical world in the civilization that He wants to manifest within this Nation of His Heart. And you, His Loved Family, may I say, I shall ever stand and guard and honor every Trust He gives Me in My Effort to help Him bring within this Nation the Perfection that is to expand here forever; for the Gifts He gives now to become a permanent part of this world will never again be touched by the discord of man. They are to remain this time as part of the Heaven on Earth that is to become the permanent condition of this world.

May My Love ever be a Mantle about you, and keep you aware of all that you can have; and your Call to the Angelic Host bring Them closer to you until They give you all that He wants you to have from Them as His Blessed Messengers of Love and Light and Purity and Freedom and Peace to the Earth.

Thank you forever for your love of the Light! Now may all that Love can give bring you greater Light, until you are able to give It to all because your own Radiation is just naturally Self-luminous wherever you abide! Thank you forever! Good night.

CHAPTER VI

MESSENGER NUMBER ONE
FROM THE
SECRET LOVE STAR

Chicago, Illinois
January 16, 1953
Record SG 1877

Beloved Ones of the Sacred Fire, We come tonight to again intensify the feeling and realization within you of that Magic Power of the Universe, that Eternal Miracle Power of Love that is the Master Control—the Master Hand that governs Manifestation that produces Perfection for all everywhere. And in entering into the use of Its Cosmic Fire, the Great Sacred Fire of Its Invincible Victory everywhere in this world, try to feel that you are becoming a part of Its Mighty Outpouring to the Earth; and at any time when you give It recognition, you can feel yourselves walking within a Ray directly from Its Presence to the Earth.

As you feel yourselves enfolded in the Great
Ray of Light from Its Heart, which is in reality
part of the Sacred Fire, there can come in and
about you a Radiance. As you intensify this by
your attention to It, It will become a Peace-com-
manding Presence to those about you. As It is
continued, there comes a soft Radiance around
the body, as you live more and more within your
Conscious Awareness of Its Mighty Outpouring
to you.

The Angelic Host from the Secret Love Star
are the Guardians of those Light Rays and those
Activities of the Sacred Fire which We direct to
the Earth. Therefore, as you ask for this to be
made a permanent part of you and your world
and invite those of the Angelic Host who are the
Guardians of this Power, you will find Them
becoming real Friends in your outer activities,
and a real, tangible Presence that often will throw
a Radiance about you that will shut off many
conditions that heretofore have seemed difficult
for you to control or to repel from your world.

The Secret Love Star is a Focus of a certain
Activity of the Sacred Fire of that Eternal Love
to the Earth, which continues to give and give
and give Its Sacred Fire into various locations in

order to be the Strengthening, Purifying, Harmonizing Activity in certain localities to hold that which is constructive in command of certain Powers in the atmosphere about you. The Light Rays from the Secret Love Star, as well as Its Sacred Fire, come to Earth to interpenetrate the consciousness of the mass of mankind, as well as their feeling world. It penetrates the physical atmosphere in the Activity of the Sacred Fire. But when the Assistance is given to those who are constructive, or trying to hold to the constructive way of Life, the Light Rays are used about an individual to gradually intensify the Luminosity of the atmosphere about the physical body, because the "Presence" of each individual—ever awaiting an opportunity to raise the vibratory action of the outer self—continually pours forth Light Rays much as you would pour water through a sponge to change its quality.

The Light Rays that come from the Secret Love Star carry within Them principally the Activity of Illumination to both the substance of the body—to the mental and feeling world—and the atmosphere itself. The Activity of the Sacred Fire from the Secret Love Star is directly projected by those who govern Its Outpouring, and

the Angelic Host are the Guardians of the Power
of that Flame, because about the Flame ever has
to be held an insulating Substance of the Love
from the Angelic Host.

There is no Activity of the Sacred Fire comes
to this Earth without the Guarding Presence of
the Angelic Host. That is to keep the Sacred Fire
insulated within the Substance of Eternal Purity
from Our Octave, and that acts as an insulation,
or a division between the energy in the atmosphere of Earth and the intensifying action of the
Sacred Fire within the Flame that is projected.

Now since the mass of mankind do not understand or know of the Reality and Blessing from
the Secret Love Star, there is not much receptiv-
ity or acknowledgment of It by conscious choice
of the free will in the mass of the people. Therefore, those of you who have been drawn under
this Radiation and have been given some explanation of this Secret Love Star—if you will give
Us this Assistance—can have individually infinitely more of Its Power than you realize.

As the Mighty Saint Germain told you, during the time of the Manifestation of Beloved Jesus
upon the Earth, the Rays from the Secret Love
Star only touched the Earth around the land of

Judea; and that was again to keep insulated the Power that came with Beloved Jesus to be that which brought the Victory of His Accomplishment into Manifestation in the physical octave. It was His Protection, and the Purifying Activity into the atmosphere in which He moved, to enable His Work to be accomplished and certain Records made in the atmosphere.

Now for the first time in the history of this world, the Rays from the Secret Love Star are enfolding the entire Earth, regardless of the hatred of mankind's generation over the past. These Light Rays are intensifying and expanding as well as enfolding the planet. Hour by hour the Light becomes brighter! Hour by hour the Sacred Fire becomes more intense in the lower atmosphere of Earth, and It must interpenetrate the ground itself in order to hold certain Forces of Nature in balanced control when certain other Activities take place.

Therefore, individually, each of you may have a Stream of that Light, or Its Enfolding Flame, as you choose, to be held ever about you for any specific purpose that you call It forth—so long as that purpose fulfills the Divine Plan and renders Service to the mass of mankind. You as individuals, <u>can have</u> individual Light Rays, or individual Flames of Its Love about you if you call that forth for the annihilation of all hate, and the release of all life from that which is not Light, is not the Love of the "Presence."

Now let Me show you! As you call this in and about yourselves and you ask your "Presence," your own "Beloved I AM Presence," to take advantage of that and use it in the most powerful way possible, many things will occur in your experiences that will surprise you greatly, but which will bless you infinitely and forever. As you are willing to make yourselves an open door for this Mighty Outpouring—individually to you, as well as to the planet, in your Calls for the Freedom of mankind from that which is not the Love of Eternity—then your "Beloved I AM Presence" is given a very much greater opportunity in Its Service to the world to intensify the Power that consumes the hate of the world.

You see, your own "Blessed I AM Presence" and Higher Mental Body are concerned, My Dear Ones, with the purifying and perfecting of the planet quite as much as with the activity of the outer self. May I say to you, the outer self is only a third of, may we say, the Business of the

"Presence"! Therefore, in Its Cosmic Service to the Nation and the world, It works with these Activities of the Sacred Fire and the Cosmic Light in ways you dream not of.

And so if by Conscious Call and remembrance of your "Presence" and Its Work to the mass of mankind, you call to the Secret Love Star and to Us to intensify daily the Light Rays or the Sacred Fire—an Individualized Flame of Its Presence in and around you by Conscious Desire, so your "Mighty I AM Presence" can take advantage of that and use It to more quickly assist the mass of the people—well, naturally, there would come to you very much greater Blessing than you can possibly realize.

In this Work which the Mighty Saint Germain has brought forth, there is always held about those under this Radiation the individualized Light Rays and those Activities of the Sacred Fire that have been brought to your attention, and which were explained to you in the beginning. If you will remember and hold the Picture of those Light Rays in and around all under this Radiation, and then the various Activities of the Sacred Fire, it makes it infinitely easier, and you may have infinitely greater Power to assist you, as you give this opportunity to your "Blessed I AM Presence" through your Conscious Desire and Call to Us.

You cannot call for one Blessing to Life and not be blessed infinitely yourselves. Sometimes, perhaps, you seem weary, and so much discord of the outer world, may I say, is sometimes heaped upon you; but after all, if you will use it instead of letting it use you, it will be a steppingstone to your mastery. Then as you take that attitude to it—that you are going to use it—well then, it will no longer disturb you! It's all in the mental and feeling world that one has the ability to change a condition from discord into harmony. And the Transmuting Power—it doesn't make any difference who likes it or doesn't—the Transmuting Power of the Universe is the use of this Sacred Fire and these Great Light Rays.

These Great Light Rays play through the atmosphere of Earth like mighty searchlights, and there are times when They cross; and where They meet, a tremendous Outpouring takes place into the structure of Earth itself. Therefore, the "I AM" Student Body are free to call these Light Rays from the Secret Love Star in and around yourselves, into your homes, into your business, and have Their Blessing that is infinite! You can call the Sacred Fire from the Secret Love Star to come in and around you and transmute your outer conditions into the Victory of God for which you have called. You can call the Individualized Flames from the Secret Love Star, and Legions of the Angelic Host to send forth that Sacred Fire into conditions that affect the mass of the people; and those Flames can take up Their permanent location in the world and begin Their complete dissolving of that which is wrong.

So your Power, My Dear Ones, and your Blessing in the use of these Great Light Rays and the Sacred Fire, is far more than you understand. And because you are so few compared to the mass of mankind, your privilege is beyond any words to describe. Only when you use this and feel and have the Blessings which It brings into your world will you understand how Great is the Service of the Angelic Host to the mankind of Earth. Mankind do not dream of the continual Blessings that come to them from the Angelic Host alone! *(applause)* Thank you, Precious Ones.

As your Mighty Saint Germain told you so long ago, there is so much stress and energy given to the outer stress of things—the outer activities of the personal self that the "Presence" doesn't care anything about—that if We can train you to discipline yourselves and concentrate your attention upon these Activities with just the natural love of the outer self to the "Presence" and to Us in the use of these Activities; well then, My Dear Ones, because the attention comes to the Sacred Fire and comes into the Light, automatically It draws that Light back to you.

You cannot even think of your "Mighty I AM Presence" or the Sacred Fire or these Light Rays, even for an instant, without Them coming back to you and blessing you infinitely more than you can possibly comprehend. One wave of love and recognition and gratitude to your "Mighty I AM Presence" or to Us brings back a thousand Rays in and around you in return for your love to Us! Therefore mankind are not without Friends; therefore mankind are not without Assistance. Therefore mankind are not at the mercy of destructive forces, if they will but return to the Greater Life of the Universe the attention of the outer self long enough to receive the Blessing of the Love that sets them Free! *(applause)* Thank you, Precious Ones.

Since you are moving in the atmosphere that is loaded with the hate and the filth and the discord of mankind, and you do not like it, well then, it is reasonable to suppose that you will turn your attention to your "Mighty I AM Presence" and to Us, and receive the Power to change the condition! If you are hungry and you need to go buy food, you go to the grocery store or the restaurant, and you have no difficulty in gathering what you want to fulfill your requirement. And since the world must have the Fire of Our Love in order to be purified from its hate, then those of you who understand this Law can call that forth into outer action, and should have no trouble feeling the Manifestation and watching It perform the Miracles in the physical world.

I want you to know how near is the Miracle Power of the Universe! I want you to know what you can have just by turning your attention to your "Presence" and to Us and making the Call! I think Life is very wonderful in the ways and means It has provided to lift mankind out of the deliberately chosen, self-created distress and degradation and dishonor. Life is very good to you, Dear Ones, very good to you! Life is far better to mankind than mankind are to life!

There is no such thing as an innocent misuse of life. Everyone deals with life every instant of Eternity and always will. Therefore, if you choose to turn your attention and your Love to your "Mighty I AM Presence" and to Our Life in the Secret Love Star, I assure you, Our Life will come back to you with all the Blessings at Our Command; and each of you could abide in a World of the Light and the Sacred Fire from the Secret Love Star. You can have It in your homes, in your minds, your bodies, your worlds, your business—you could move insulated in that at all times if you so choose to make the Call!

So in entering into this Explanation tonight, it is with the hope that you may become more and more aware of the Magnificent Beings from the Secret Love Star whose Love to the Earth could melt mankind's human creation almost overnight, if the mass of the people knew and would love and call to the Source that can set them Free. Life is full of Miracle Powers, and We have offered Them day after day after day through these Dictations—and the Great Angelic Host and the Cosmic Beings and the Ascended Ones offered you solution after solution of your outer problems. You have had Blessing after

Blessing without limit, and there is an infinite amount more! There's no limitation to the Blessings of the Universe! There is nothing to say you nay when you come through Love. All it takes is for you to open the door from your side of life by love to the Greater Life, to have everything the Greater Life has to flood into your world and make you master over the limitations here.

You will never find a substitute for the Greater Life and the Greater Love of those Beings who are the Guardians of the Earth and the Saviors of mankind. You may search the world over. You may think for Eternity, and unless Love from the Unfed Flame in your Heart comes to the Greater Life in the Universe—the Greater Activity of the Sacred Fire—the Expanding Power of Life cannot go on. The natural Expansion of the Unfed Flame in your Hearts, which is the Expansion of the Perfection of the Universe from within your own life, cannot go on without the assisting Love of the Greater Life.

So since you have been held within the Glory and the Blessings of the Secret Love Star ever since the Mighty Saint Germain brought this Light forth, you have been cradled, as it were,

within the Light Rays and the Sacred Fire of Our
Love. If you will call It into action in and around
yourselves, and then demand that Its Authority
be the only Authority in the outer world of
mankind, that hate may cease to be and the
shadows of human distress be annihilated, then
your willingness to draw that into outer action
will automatically perfect you and your world.

Your world has to be perfected by the Sacred
Fire of Our Love, and if it were not so, you
would have been perfected long ago. It matters
not who wants to do it or who doesn't want to!
It doesn't make any difference who agrees with
Us or doesn't agree with Us. There's only one
thing that can stop distress and put Perfection in
its place forever, and that is the Sacred Fire of
Eternal Love. *(applause)* Thank you, Precious
Ones.

When you understand how deep is the Feeling
of that Sacred Fire within your own Life, and you
begin to feel Its Power surge through you
instantly at your command, you will begin to
know that the Mastery of life is the use of the
Sacred Fire of Eternal Love. No matter what your
problems are, the Sacred Fire of Eternal Love is
your Mastery over them. Be it individual,

national or worldwide, the Sacred Fire from Our Octave has got to come into yours if conditions are to be corrected. And the only Authority and Power in the Universe which can use that kind of Force and produce the Sacred Fire in physical conditions is the Immortal Love of Our Octave and the Central Sun.

So go forward and use It, knowing It is All-powerful; and It can manifest in any Activity of the Sacred Fire necessary to purify the substance and the energy that has been contaminated by mankind's discord. As you understand the Blessings that are yours from the Secret Love Star, I trust We can come to you more frequently, come to you closer, and clothe you with Greater Power of the Sacred Fire to let your "Mighty I AM Presence" and Higher Mental Body of each Life Stream render the Fullness of Its Service in assisting the Mighty Saint Germain to cleanse the Nation, and through the Nation, cleanse the world—because if it is not cleansed by Conscious Command and the Call of the Hearts of individuals, then the Cosmic Law must cleanse it in ways that compel Purification.

But the human creation causes the distress that is indescribable! When mankind throughout the

ages have built the accumulation and the creation
that, may I say, infest the world at this time, then
surely you must know that the Cosmic Law does
not indefinitely allow the atmosphere of Earth to
be saturated with destruction, with filth, and with
desecration.

Therefore, every Call you make—to draw the
Cosmic Power of the Secret Love Star's Mighty
Flame of Eternal Love into physical conditions—
is just that much Raising, Transmuting, Purifying
Activity that goes on in you and your world, and
then floods out to the Nation and the Earth. And
in this way you can bring tremendous relief to
many Life Streams that otherwise would have to
endure terrific suffering.

You have the Power to use this Great Mercy
of Life to reduce the suffering of mankind! And
so I come to assist you, and to remind you of the
Sacred Fire that is ever by your side for your use
by Conscious Call. And It is the Miracle Love of
Eternity that will forever produce Perfection at
your Command! *(applause, audience standing)*
Thank you so much, Precious Ones.

Now for just a moment, if you care to hold
this Picture of a Golden Sun through which plays
the Pink and the Violet Flames, and you accept

that you move in a Sphere of Its Presence, then
We can establish this about you—if you make the
Call for Its Focus to be held about you from the
Secret Love Star. Then as the Power of that Love
and Its Sacred Fire increases around you, there
can come those of the Angelic Host which guard
Its Accumulating Power, until you feel the Full-
ness of Its Victory answer you instantly at your
Command.

We are ready to bring this in and about you
as you make the Call; and I ask you to feel,
sometime each day, that you move in Its
Presence, and It forever loves you and loves to
set you Free. And you in turn will love to use
Its Sacred Fire to set others Free, as you feel
your own Freedom coming in the awareness of
Its Presence. Go forward and know that It is
your Invincible God Victory manifest at your
Conscious Call to hold Protection and take you
forward to assist others as powerfully as possible,
until the Great Cosmic Law takes all in hand for
the adjustment of that which Love alone can
bring. Thank you, and won't you be seated.

May the Glory of Its Sacred Fire become visible about you. May the Radiance of Its Blazing
Light take you forward to Freedom, and may Its

Everlasting Love bring within you the great realization that to set life Free by the Miracle of the Sacred Fire of Eternal Love is the supreme privilege of unascended beings; as they send that Love to the "Mighty I AM Presence" and the Ascended Host for the Freedom of all mankind, and the Release of Life everywhere in this world from that which is not the Love of Eternity!

Go forward and know We ever stand ready to answer your every Call with Victory which is yours forever. Thank you and good night.

CHAPTER VII

BELOVED LISTENING ANGEL

Chicago, Illinois
January 2, 1954
Record CD160

Beloved Ones of God's Heart, I come in response to the Request of the Cosmic Law, and I bring to you Activities of the Angelic Host that I trust will make your way easier and leave with you the Blessings that Love wants you to have. May you feel the Reality and the Power of those Activities of the Angelic Host which are ever awaiting an opportunity to bring Manifestations into the physical world that establish Perfection for Eternity. Great is the Love of those Mighty Beings! And Great is the opportunity for Their Assistance to mankind when some will give Them the attention of the outer self—and the Call of the Heart for Their Love from Their Realm of Life—to come and abide with the children of

Earth, that they may know what the Love of the Mighty Heart of Creation means to the universe around them.

It is My Privilege to open the Door into Our Realm of Light. I trust you will be conscious of Its more Dazzling Presence ever about you. May you feel Its Healing Radiance and Love to command in this world all that you contact to yield to you the Perfection of God. The Realm of the Angelic Host is Magnificent and Beautiful and Powerful beyond anything that We can describe to you; but We want you to feel, *through your own feeling world,* the Power of Our Light which is Our Love from the Great Central Sun brought to Earth to assist those who look Godward and are trying to reach up and hold to Perfection. The Power of the Angelic Host is that always of Love, and the Sacred Fire which is the Concentration of that Love into outer action comes forth ever at Our Command to render Assistance wherever possible.

And now, since it is My Privilege to have come into the lower atmosphere of Earth, I bring to you the Blessings and the awareness of those of the Angels and the other Beings of the Angelic Host who are awaiting an opportunity to clothe you with Power for more conscious cooperation. I trust you will feel Our nearness! I trust you will use the Light of Our Love in your outer activities; and I trust We shall make you feel Our Presence frequently, even in the midst of outer turmoil. The Sacred Fire and the Eternal Light of the Love from Our Great Realm of Life is ever seeking an onward Path through mankind in this world, where We may establish Our Perfection to take Its Dominion in the outer world's activities until all behold Us face to face.

In the Mighty Blessings that have come to you from the Magnificent Beings who have loved you so much, and loved you so long, and have been so patient with you throughout the ages; those Beloved Ones have called Us into outer action to more quickly fulfill your Calls and to establish a stronger Guard about your activities. From the Heights of Creation ever flows the Light of Eternal Love, and because mankind have created shadows in the human distress of the outer world, then the hour strikes when there must come from Heights incalculable the descent of the Beings of the Sacred Fire, the descent of the Light of Eternal Love, and the descent of Power that is at once—instantly in full Command. So as We offer

you from Our Great Realm the Power of the Angelic Host, try to feel It very tangible within your
own feeling world. Try to absorb It and feel the
Light of Our Power. Try to dwell within It, even
though in the midst of outer chaos; and you will
find ever abiding by your side those Beings who
love you and who love to protect you as you move
forward in greater activity to release the blessings
that you are yet to give to mankind en masse.

You are the Open Door through whom Great
Blessings will come to the people of Earth, and
I am one of the Guardians of that Door. At the
present time I guard It alone, but there are others, who are in Cosmic capacity, also the Guard
of that Open Door if a Guard is required. *You rep-
resent that Open Door to mankind,* so there must flow
through that the Light from Our Octave that Love
alone creates. So if you listen for the Harmonies
from Our Octave, as you hear Them, you will see
the Light. Our Love sings Its way through Creation and ever produces the Luminous Beauty of
everything that will bless mankind. And not one
shadow comes forth from those who dwell within
Our Realm!

For almost five years I have been waiting for
this opportunity; and so My Love has increased

during that time, as has My Desire to pour It forth to you for outer use. I trust you will not forget to use It and remember Me in My Offer for Its Release to the Earth and to you all! *(ap-plause)* Thank you, Precious Ones, with all My Heart. Won't you be seated, please. Love must come from Great Cosmic Heights at this time in the shape of the Sacred Fire, and as you have called this forth into outer physical conditions, We have watched your Desire expand and your determination to call this forth ever increase through your Conscious Calls. Therefore, We are adding now to your Calls the Release of more of this Power that must come into physical conditions if they are to be purified and corrected.

The Angelic Host are the Bearers of the Sacred Fire as well as the Great Light Rays from Cosmic Heights of Life's tremendous Activity. And so when mankind need Us, We come and offer Our Love, for We know naught but Its Service to Life. And wherever We abide, We are clothed in Its Light into which no discord can enter. Now We offer you the Light of Our Love to enfold you, that you may have more Power with which to render Service, that you may have more Protection against the shadows, and

that you may have more Illumination to reveal
to you ahead of time the things you will need to
know.

If you understood how wondrous are the Activities and the Service of the Angelic Host, you
would want to remember Them hourly! I bless
you all for giving Us as much recognition as you
have. The more you recognize Us, the more We
will recognize you; and We will hold the balance
thus in outer conditions by Our Response to your
Call to Us. Do not feel that We are far away! Do
not feel that it takes time for Us to come! Swifter
than Light is the quick Descent of Our Presence
at your Call—from Heights indescribable to the
mind of man. And when you understand the
Oneness of God's Life and the Sacred Fire of
Eternal Love, you will know that Its quick Descent in response to your Call is practically
instantaneous.

You might wonder how We know of your
Call. Since We know of your Life and your
existence, and since We are One with your
"Beloved I AM Presence," there is not a breath
apart when that Cosmic Love moves into action
to accomplish Its Mighty Purpose of purifying
the Earth and raising all that is constructive into

greater Expansion and greater Service and greater Blessing to the universe around you. I have listened for a long while for the Call from the Hearts of the people of Earth. I have listened a long time, and I have ever been ready to answer every Call. And since the Calls have come to Us through the Mighty Saint Germain's "I AM" Activities, We are ever ready to hold the Guard about you and clothe you with everything that will enable you to serve Him more wondrously in your outer world.

And may I say to you, there is nothing the outer world requires quite so much at this time as Our Presence. Little does mankind understand the Power We wield, the Service We offer, and the Love We can bestow. We have been denied and defied through the centuries—and yet We have been recognized and loved and worshipped through the centuries; and so We ever seek through those who know of Our Reality to bring about the Blessings that will enable the rest of mankind to be absolutely certain of Our Presence, accept Our Reality, and give Us the cooperation by which We may help all. After all, everything that is constructive on Earth today needs Our Guarding Presence to protect it; and so those who are reaching to the constructive way of Life are naturally the ones to whom We come first and offer the best We have.

From Heights of Power unbelievable to the human intellect there can come Assistance to you all in times when some of you scarcely know you need it. Yet I say to you, every moment you need the Light of Our Love to abide with you, to travel with you, to dwell within you, and to expand through and around you in order to keep the Blessings and the Power from Our Octave ever flowing in and around you until your Service to Life is finished in this world. You have called for greater Protection, and so the Call has been answered by those of Us who have the Power to protect, who know how to protect, and who, to a very large degree, can tell you ahead of time when you are going to need that Protection. So your awareness of Our Presence with you will automatically enable Our Protection to abide with you. And may Our Flame of Love stand between you and everything of the outer world's disturbance.

We can bring you Power of Accomplishment which comes from Love alone—not the love as you know it—the Love from the Great Central

Sun that bestows Its Boundless Power and Infinite Perfection upon the extension of Itself, upon each Life Flame who will open the Door and let the Blessings flow. So now, since I have been Guardian of that Door—and which I still am—I offer you tonight the opportunity for It to swing wide so far as each of you is concerned, and let the Blessings of Our Realm flood you and your world for your use in very practical ways. The Angelic Host are going to manifest to mankind in ways that cannot be denied! *(applause)* Thank you, Precious Ones. For just a moment while you are standing, I wish to say, some of those Manifestations are to come through the Pageant and moving picture of "I AM" COME! because you have given Us the Opportunity and have opened the Door by which We may act in your world to bless you, and through you bring to mankind the proof of Our Reality, the Release of Our Power, and the Light of Our Enfolding Love that all shall see and all shall feel, and one day, all must be. Thank you. Won't you be seated, please.

In entering into the lower atmosphere of Earth tonight, it is with Great Happiness that I can make you aware of Myself in a very Tangible, Powerful Way. I hope and I feel certain that you will be aware of My Presence—and the Presence of others of the Angelic Host—quite tangibly, perhaps several times each day. If We can dwell together in the Release of this Power and Light of Our Love, you will find growing rapidly in the mental and feeling world of mankind the acceptance of Our Presence and the Call for Our Help. And this is what We require to render still greater Assistance. So We have come to you as the Open Door through which We may all release to the Earth the Sacred Fire of Eternal Love whose Miracles will never cease, and whose Miracles are All-powerful everywhere throughout the Universe.

The Door I hold open tonight invites you into Our Realm during the time when the body rests in sleep. If you ask to come, We can give you Assistance which you will feel when you awaken in the morning. In the tangible, physical flesh body you will feel the Power, the Reality, the Love, and the Peace which enters into you as you come to Us each night and dwell within Our Realm of Power and Light and Love and Peace. And as you bring It back into the outer self will you find the day giving you Its Blessings with a great joy. Each day will be the anticipation of greater joy, until you will find that the Love of the Angelic Host is the Daystar that leads you to Heights without limit, and to Peace Eternal, and clothes you with Power to do anything; so long as the Great "God Presence," the "Mighty I AM," is loved and worshipped and recognized and obeyed.

So as we enter into closer association through the production of "I AM" COME! you will find more of Our Blessings ever attending you, and all of Our Power ever ready to assist you as you go forward and reveal to the world the Beauty and the Power and the Love of the Beings in Our Realm of Life. May Our Realm and yours become One now; and as the greater Expansion of this Activity of the Mighty Saint Germain reaches into the Hearts and minds of mankind, it will carry the conviction of Our Reality and Our Love and Our Ever-blessing Presence to abide with those who begin to recognize Our Existence and Our Power to assist mankind to be Free. There are many Beings in the Realms of the Angelic Host whose Beauty will make you speechless with Love and Adoration because It blesses with such Power that It brings those Beings close to you. And then again, once more you will live in God's World of the Happiness and the Purity and the Love that is your Eternal Heritage.

May you feel the Peace of My Love and the Power of Its Light ever clothing you at all times with whatever you require, until abiding with you, It becomes your world forever. May you forever, forever, and forever dwell in the Heart of My Love and be Its Victorious Command to the Earth wherever you abide, until It illumines everything with the Light of Eternity. Thank you with all My Heart.

CHAPTER VIII

BELOVED GODFRE

Shasta Springs, California
September 3, 1956
Record CD 290

Dear Hearts of the Light, tonight in releasing the Greater Illumination which must come to those under this Radiation, I wish to call your attention again to the Reminder We gave long ago in the beginning of this "I AM" Activity. It was the first Guard that Beloved Saint Germain set up for Us in the beginning of this Work when We first began to receive the Dictations. HIS FIRST WARNING TO US WAS THAT WHEN YOU SEE ANYTHING AT THE INNER LEVEL THAT IS NOT SURROUNDED BY BLAZING LIGHT, DO NOT ACCEPT IT INTO YOUR WORLD, AND COMMAND AND ORDER IT ANNIHILATED!

The reason for that is this: Anything that comes from your "Mighty I AM Presence" or Higher

Mental Body has to come in Blazing White Light because It is not composed of anything but Light, and therefore Its Natural Radiation is that of Light. Anything that comes from an Ascended Master or Cosmic Being or the Angelic Host is always held within an Oval of Blazing White Light because there is nothing of the shadows in Our Octave. There is Light within Light!—greater Light, more intense Light, always surrounded by more Light. *Therefore when people say they see the Ascended Masters, unless what they see is seen in Blazing White Light, they are only seeing their own thought forms and their own concept of the Master. I want to make this clear, because the psychic forces have fooled mankind down through the centuries.* Unless your "Mighty I AM Presence" and the Ascended Masters show you something in Blazing White Light, don't accept it! Your own "Presence" is Light, and It cannot create a shadow. The Ascended Masters' Bodies are made of Cosmic Light Substance which does not create a shadow. Now if you don't want to believe Me, then certainly your experiences are going to bring you agony untold, but I must make this clear. The Truth must be known, and that which is revealed within Blazing Light is the Truth.

So don't go around telling people what you see unless you see it in Blazing White Light—and then it is more for your own Instruction than it is for someone else. Every individual has the capacity within the Life Stream, if the outer self is kept purified, to see within that Life Stream directly to the "Mighty I AM Presence" or Higher Mental Body. You have the capacity within Life to see the Ascended Masters and Angelic Host, provided there is no impurity in your own mental and feeling world or the atmosphere about you or your flesh body. Therefore, Life has provided the way of showing you within the Light the true condition of everything. What cannot create a Light and manifest a Light to you certainly is no friend of yours and never will bring you anything but mistakes and mistaken concepts—which will bind you longer—until the Light becomes the World of Eternal Truth about you. So I offer this tonight for your acceptance. If you prefer to be entertained by seeing your own thought forms, your concepts, being your own creation, do not necessarily tell you the Truth. And unless those concepts are in Blazing Light, they are but human creation.

Now there are a lot of people who don't want to believe Me. They think they know more than the Ascended Host, and a good many of them think they know more than what's in the rest of the Universe; but that is the human creation, the human ego of conceit and pride and arrogance and ignorance which drives people to the second death. I am offering you the Blazing White Light of Eternal Truth! It will never lie to you! It will never give you a problem! It will never give you anything but the Blessings of Love and Eternal Perfection. I will try to stand your Guard if you care to accept what I have said. *(applause)* Thank you so much, Precious Ones. Won't you be seated, please.

My Purpose in bringing this to you tonight is not for any personal reason. I am trying to concentrate this Knowledge to you and this Infallible Truth and Power of the Law from Our Octave, that the hordes of evil may not be able to connect with you to impose either a hypnotic control or force you into the condition of brainwashing. Now I have offered this for your own Protection. The Messenger has nothing to do with it, except to reveal the Truth I bring. She has called for the Invincible Purity of Eternal Truth, and the Sacred

Fire of that Eternal Truth shall blaze till that Truth is known everywhere. That Truth and the Sacred Fire must surround you if you are to be insulated and cut free from any connection with the hordes of evil in the outer world that are using the most depraved suggestions to bring mankind under their devilish control.

So if I may assist you tonight, I certainly can be your Protector. If I were you, I would be dynamite on constantly charging around you the Blazing White Light of the Ascended Masters' Eternal Purity, the Blazing White Light of the Ascended Masters' Eternal Truth; and let the Sacred Fire's Eternal Truth fill you and surround you with Its Dazzling White Light until the hordes of evil take the consequences. There are forces in the atmosphere of which none of mankind know. We see them acting constantly. But unless you are insulated in a Light so bright they cannot see who abides within, you become a target of their viciousness—because they hate the Light.

It is My Privilege in the Service to Beloved Saint Germain to try to guard you with every bit of information the Cosmic Law will permit Us to give. So no matter what you see in the sleeping state or in the waking state, unless you see what

you see in Blazing Light or in a Sacred Fire—
which never produces a red glow—what you see,
unless it is in Dazzling White Light, should be
blasted out of your world. Now I am trying with
everything I know how to hold Protection around
those under this Radiation if they will let Me. But
your part of the Power of Protection is to, with
every atom of your being, when anything is shown
to you that is not in Blazing Light, demand its
annihilation from the Universe, because it does
not come from either your Higher Mental Body
or the Ascended Host; therefore it is not of the
Christ.

I want to explain something about this Messenger. When she asks for Truth or Illumination,
We flash the Light, and she does not give out
anything unless the Light has been flashed. (applause) Thank you, Precious Ones. Won't you be
seated, please. For over thirty years she has been
shown the Light—Blazing Suns of Light larger
than this room. Suns of Light have stood within
the room where her body lay wide awake. That
was the preparation of the outer self before this
knowledge of the "I AM" came forth from the
Mighty Saint Germain. Let no one expect Our
Help that doubts what the Light has shown her!

Now she stands your champion, as do the rest of Us; but I tell you frankly, if it be necessary, which I hope it is not, to shock certain destructive forces by a release of Light that will shake the bodies until the doubt is gone; if We have to do it, We will do it! But I hope it does not have to be the experience of anyone who has been loved and brought into the Light thus far. So I send the warning to the defiant forces that have doubted the Light that is the Strength to carry the responsibility that serves only the Light. Blessed Ones, "I AM" your Champion; and from tonight, if you will be dynamite against everything that is not the Ascended Masters' Truth of Eternal Light, the Ascended Masters' Invincible Truth of the Sacred Fire, the Ascended Masters' Invincible Sacred Fire Control of all you ever contact, that Sacred Fire will enfold you. Within It is the Light which will reveal to you, Inner and outer, whatever is necessary for you to know from time to time. And that will as certainly protect you and supply you and heal you as you give It recognition and call It into action.

It is a Gift that the whole world put together cannot give. But the Ascended Hosts are necessary for mankind's Freedom; otherwise We would have gone on centuries agone to Higher Accomplishment and the creation of systems of worlds. Don't let anyone under this Radiation get so arrogant as to say, "Well, I have my 'Mighty I AM Presence'! I don't need you or the Ascended Host!" You've had your "I AM Presence" all through the ages, and you forgot you even had It; and you did not even know the Ascended Masters existed until the Mighty Saint Germain brought this Light!

So Blessed Ones, when arrogance arises, the shadows enfold. Now I am here to bring the Light of all the Love the world requires—Light enough to annihilate the hate of the world! Light enough to purify everything in existence can come at Our Command to lift mankind out of the clutches of their own destructive creation until that creation can be consumed from the Universe, never to touch any other part of Life. So as you go forward and accomplish greater and greater Victories in that Light, fail not to hold the Picture of the Sun of Dazzling Light. Now it can be white or silver or gold. It can be violet or blue, occasionally pink.

Now if you will demand of anything that is shown, "IN THE NAME OF THE 'MIGHTY I AM

PRESENCE,' IN THE NAME OF THE ASCENDED
JESUS CHRIST! **SHOW ME YOUR LIGHT!**" And
if that which you see cannot show you a Light,
then it is but the manifestation of the hordes of
evil pretending to be the Truth of the Light. We
have given you an infallible means of protecting
yourselves and of testing everything that comes
to your consciousness; and if you will take your
stand to forbid anything to look in your direction
but that which is the Truth and the Legions of
Light, you will find the Christ in and around you—
which your Higher Mental Body is—holds the
Cosmic Christ Victory in you, your world, and
your affairs. Now this is a Powerful Strengthening
Activity as well as a Protection and an Illumination and a Safeguard against being fooled by
hypnotic forces that pretend to be the Real—until
they have caught mankind in their clutches and
are on the way to destruction.

We are trying with everything the Cosmic
Law permits to hold the "I AM" Student Body
protected; and the only Protection of that which
is constructive is the Power of Light, the Power
of the Sacred Fire. The Sacred Fire does not
permit the human to survive. The Light, the
Cosmic Light which We project, the Light from

the Higher Mental Body, does not permit any shadow to come within It; therefore, it is the annihilation of that which is of human creation.

So from tonight, if you will accept My Explanation of holding about you not only your Tube of Light and the World of the Violet Consuming Flame, but holding about yourselves by conscious recognition and by your love for It, a Blazing Sun Presence of the Light of Eternal Truth—the Cosmic Light of the Cosmic Christ Truth. Feel your world filled with that Blazing Sun Presence, and demand that the Perfection of the Ascended Host fill and surround you and your world; and within It is automatically released to you the supply of anything you will ever require. We could long ago have given this to you; but until you come to a certain point of fierce determination to have nothing to do with that which is of the shadows, some of these Inner Activities must be held in abeyance until your own Higher Mental Body has released a certain intensity of that Light in and around you by which you recognize what It is doing for you; and then cooperate with It by calling forth the Sun Presence of the Cosmic Christ Light in which that which is of the shadows can never come or even approach.

So Blessed Ones, let Us clear the decks, release the Cosmic Light of the Cosmic Christ, demand Its Invincible Victory and Protection around those under this Radiation, and demand Its Intensification every day in everything you do, till It is just a natural outflow of that Cosmic Christ Light of Eternal Truth filling you and your world with Perfection, and letting It expand until It crowds back the hordes of the shadows until those hordes are consumed.

Now you can use this—the same idea of the Blazing Sun Presence within which is any Ascended Master's Form or Likeness—to enfold those in your government, those in the National Defense or the Civil Defense or any special activity within your Land. The people must have Light, My Dear Ones, if they are going to find their way out of the shadows and into the Freedom of the Ascended Host! So unless the Light is recognized and called into concentrated action in and around an individual, It ever remains in Its Cosmic Flow; and the individual stays within a world of human concepts until the Cosmic Light comes and consumes those concepts. So in offering this to you, it is not only to clear your own consciousness and safeguard you in your experiences; it is to fill your world with Its Perfection and clothe you in the Sun Presence of a Power to help others; and wherever you go, allow that Light to expand and intensify until It reaches the Cosmic Action that annihilates the hordes of evil before they can approach.

When the Great Cosmic Law intensifies the Release through this whole system of worlds of more Violet Consuming Flame and more of this Cosmic Light Substance, It will pass through all the planets in this system. It will pass through everybody and everything on every planet and release more Light through all manifestation in this system. But you individually do not need to wait for that forward impulse in Its Great Cosmic Cyclic Action. You may have this intensified every day the moment you begin to call for It, to hold your attention upon It, to love It in and around you until It becomes the World of the Cosmic Christ enfolding you in the Ascended Masters' Victory of Cosmic Christ Control.

That is why, in the distress Call of the Great White Brotherhood that, *"THE LIGHT OF GOD NEVER FAILS!"* it is because, My Dear Ones, the moment you speak those Words, your Higher Mental Body and some Ascended Master will

immediately release Light in and around you
whenever you ask for It. And I don't know of any
Greater Blessing and Assurance that can come to
mankind than that *the Light is always ready to give
you Itself whenever you ask for It.* You cannot remain
in the darkness when you ask for the Light. You
cannot remain in distress if the Light fills you and
your world. You cannot have distress in your
country if the Light is called by the people to
come into the country and fill the country with
the Cosmic Christ–which that Light is.

Beloved Ones, there is no such thing as not
attaining your Victory once you learn to dwell
within the Sun of the Everlasting Light of the
Cosmic Christ. This is your Privilege! This is the
Knowledge all mankind should have had long
ago, and could have had if they had been through
with the shadows. But you can't face the Light
one moment and turn your back on It the next;
for when you look into the shadows, you move
and are drawn into them. When you look into the
Light and ask the Light to surround you, then
you become that Light!

So Beloved Ones, tonight as you are entering
into these Decrees to help purify the Nation in
the coming election, as you call forth the Sun of

Cosmic Christ Light and Its Eternal Purity to fill this Nation, hold the Picture of that Sun filling the Land. Each of you who is here from a foreign land can do the same thing for your own country. Whenever you think of it and decree for the correction of conditions, hold the Picture of the Cosmic Sun of Cosmic Christ Light descending into the Nation, filling it until there is nothing remains but that Sun of Cosmic Christ Perfection. If mankind but recognizes this Light and loves It and calls It into outer conditions, the Light automatically is released and begins to flow in and around you, or into the condition whenever you send the Call.

The Cosmic Law is such that when you ask for Light, Light must be given. That is why the admonition through the centuries has been given to mankind, *"Call unto Me and I will answer thee!"* The Light has said, *"Ask for Light and you shall receive Light!"* Place your attention upon the Light, and the Light begins to fill you, and you become all Light. If you want the atmosphere about you Light, ask the Light to illumine the atmosphere about you, and that atmosphere will become luminous. This is just as certain to manifest as that you make the Call. Unless the Light is called forth and loved, and mankind understand what is within It, It is abiding always quiescent in the atmosphere of Earth—especially the upper atmosphere—and can only be concentrated in and around and through the individual by Conscious Call, by Conscious Love, by Conscious Command for Its Concentration to come as the Cosmic Christ and hold Its Victory and Dominion in and around the outer self, or into your affairs or into the world.

But you must see the Picture of the Light if the Light is to anchor in and around you! And I assure you, the shadows will never give you what is within the Light. The Light is the Christ! The Light is the Gift and the Love from the Higher Mental Body. It is the Gift and the Love and the Perfection from the Ascended Masters' Octave. It is the Concentration of Power from the Physical Sun and the Great Central Sun. It is the Treasure House of all the Powers of Life, and It is the Heart of Eternal Truth. It comes forth from the "Mighty I AM Presence" and is the Extension of the Outpouring of Its Love, within which is all of everything to produce Perfection, to help the outer self turn from distress, and enter into the Heaven of Life's own Gift to mankind.

When you ask for the Light of the Angelic Host to fill you and your world, then the Love from the Angelic Host through the Sacred Fire flows within that Light and is held about you as a Garment of Protection, a Wall of Invincible Protection, and the Power of Victorious Accomplishment. So during the rest of this Conclave, will you, sometime each day, give recognition to the Light and the Sacred Fire which the Angelic Host are privileged to concentrate and give to mankind—for the Assistance which the Angelic Host alone convey. It is Their Service to Life at this time. They are the Custodians of Its Power. If you ask for the Light and the Sacred Fire of the Love from the Ascended Host to blaze a Sun of Their Presence around you, you will find Their Presence there—very real, very tangible— Their Gifts and Their Control flooding your world with the Perfection which They can bestow.

Blessed Ones, in entering in now to the use of the Sun Presence of the Sacred Fire and Cosmic Light of the Angelic Host, try to feel Its Intense Radiation in and around you. And if you become quiet enough, there comes a thrill in the Stillness of that Sacred Fire that is as real as reality can ever be, and will only leave in you and your world the Blessings of the Love of the Angelic Host. Tonight may Their Sun Presence of Their Hearts Flame's Love enfold each of you, your beings and worlds, your loved ones, all you hold near and dear in this world—or even in the Octave of Light—until the Blazing Power of the Angelic Host's Invincible Victory in this world becomes your World in which you live until the moment of your Ascension. This also will assist you in the hour of your Ascension because of Its Raising Power of the Sacred Fire within the Love of the Angelic Host as They offer to you Their Gifts of the Cosmic Christ.

So I enfold you tonight in such Love from the Angelic Host, in such a World of Their Perfection, that It becomes an Eternal Part of your Life Streams if you recognize It every day, and dwell within It by Conscious Command; until these Beings reveal Themselves to you face to face in Blazing Light—Their own Bodies a brighter Light; until one day you will touch Them, and Their Tangible Bodies are as visible and tangible and solid as yours. You may touch the Angelic Host! And when They touch you, Healing is complete on the instant; for the Angels of the Healing

Flame bring the World of Their Purity and Love in the Sacred Fire's Power in which naught else can exist. And They are ever ready to assist in the Healing of the individuals or the nations or the world.

So as you dwell within Their World of the Sacred Fire and you feel Their Tangible Presence with you, it will not be long until They can reveal Themselves within the Light of the Cosmic Christ; and you will know the Cosmic Christ has come to Earth to dwell with those who are to be carried forward to their Ascension. May you feel the enfolding World of the Sacred Fire of the Angelic Host and Its Cosmic Christ Victory lift you to Freedom wherever you abide. May the Fullness of Its Boundless Supply ever bless you with Eternal Perfection. Thank you with all My Heart.

"I AM" ANGEL BELLS

May Da Camara 1945

CHAPTER IX

BELOVED SAINT GERMAIN

Detroit, Michigan
June 8, 1957
Record CD 1658

Beloved Hearts of Detroit, I bring you Greetings from Heights of Purity and Love and Happiness. I trust you will come closer and closer into the Great Powerhouse of Our Use of the Sacred Fire and the awareness of Our Presence with you. Tonight I want to bring to your attention again certain Activities of the Angelic Host that you are privileged to have, that you will require as time goes on, and that are ready awaiting an opportunity to bring their Blessings to you and the world. Ordinarily, in your experience Life, as you go through a day's activities you feel as a rule that you, as an individual, are alone. It would be well if you would remind the outer self several times a day that the Higher

Mental Body stands above you, sometimes very close when your Adoration is going to the "I AM Presence" and to the Ascended Host.

The Angelic Host are ready to accompany you in your outer service of Life and to draw around you that which you're going to require in your association with your fellowman, and give you Help to give you the Power by which you not only master conditions, but by which you attain within yourselves a greater expansion of the Sacred Fire to make you more completely aware of God's Master Control of all in this world. At first it begins in small things. You'll have this and that accomplishment, and you're very happy. But you do not always give recognition to the Inner Power that has enabled you to accomplish what you desire. If you can remember, and you can if you so command it, to acknowledge always your "Beloved I AM Presence" first whenever you accomplish something successfully, and then give acknowledgement to the Angelic Host—who at the Inner Level are always assisting in every constructive activity of Life.

You do not quite understand but in a small way how closely the Angelic Host are operating or assisting you in any constructive accomplish-

ment. Now those of the Angelic Host who have
never embodied are, of course, under Our Direction. They wait for Our Direction to come and
give Assistance. But those who are Ascended
Beings, seeing your effort to hold to the Light
and bring forth that which blesses Life, are also
always awaiting an opportunity to pour forth
through you the Radiation into outer physical
conditions that not only makes your pathway
easier, but anchors in and around you more of
the Substance from the Ascended Masters' Octave which, as time goes on, is built into that
which will one day be your world of manifestation.

Now the Angelic Host—I'm speaking of those
who are not yet Ascended—handle Great Streams
of Cosmic Light Substance and draw It from time
to time in concentrated Action wherever it is
possible to hold Protection for that which is constructive. Now you might say to Me, "Well, why
can't They always hold Protection for that which
is constructive?" Because mankind—I am speaking of individuals—who by conscious command
and conscious choice select to do a certain thing
in Life, and go into that to accomplish it without
ever giving recognition to either the "Mighty

I AM Presence" or God, as the outer world knows It, or to the Angelic Host who are the Beings provided by the Cosmic Law to help the outer self do what is right.

That is why there has been down through the centuries a certain acceptance of the Angelic Host by mankind of a Guardian Angel in rare occasions of great danger—crisis—something of that sort. But if human beings only knew what they could have, only knew what the Angelic Host could do for them by accepting Their Presence with you at all times, your pathway would be infinitely easier, and what has been human struggle in the past would be joyous Activity and Victorious Accomplishment always.

Now the Angelic Host are not concerned with simply gratifying mankind's desires—not at all. Their Service is to expand the Sacred Fire of Their Love to Life. Wherever They are recognized or called into Assistance and loved and given conscious acceptance, They will always pour forth through you Their Expanding Sacred Fire Love, and It will always produce Perfection and Protection for you. So the Gift They have to give you is that which unascended beings can-

not give you. And if you care to experiment with
My Violet Flame Angels in this respect, I think
you will have some very delightful experiences!
Now several times in the past I have called attention to the Angels of the Violet Consuming
Flame, and long ago offered an Angel of the
Violet Flame to abide with you to help you use
that Violet Consuming Flame to greater Victorious Accomplishment. Now, because of the
outer world's needs, you can just as well have
a Group of Violet Flame Angels assisting you in
whatever your outer world activity is—with your
own Conscious Call for the Expansion of the
Sacred Fire of your own Life Stream into outer
world conditions. Then the Angelic Host, pouring Their Sacred Fire into that, will intensify
your Radiation until It becomes very powerful to
heal, to bless, to purify, to illumine, and to raise
all that you contact. It will make you a greater
Blessing to Life, will give you a greater sense of
Mastery over conditions, and will continually
help you to expand the Sacred Fire Power till It
fills your world with Its Perfection.

Now it takes your conscious remembrance of
Their Presence, or invitation to a Group of Violet
Flame Angels to attend you in whatever you wish

to accomplish that affects the welfare of mankind. If you care to have Them in closer and closer association, as time goes on, We can increase the Groups that will minister with you so that your own Radiation expands much more quickly and becomes much more Powerful in your assistance to Life. Now whether you wish to bless the plant life, the Life in the atmosphere, the Beings of the Elements, your fellowman—Life wherever you contact it—matters not. The Law of Perfection is the Expansion of the Life Flame, the Unfed Flame in the Heart, and as Its Radiation goes forth, Wave after Wave of that expanding Sacred Fire pours forth a Substance, just like a radiator pours forth heat, and just like the filament in the electric light bulb pours forth a light, so does the Unfed Flame in your Heart give forth a Light Substance, which is the Radiation from your emotional body, your Higher Mental Body, and into the atmosphere about you.

The greater the Purity within the individual that is maintained, the greater is the expansion of the Unfed Flame, and naturally, the greater is the Radiation of the Substance into the atmosphere about you wherever you abide. Now I have a very serious reason for offering this to you tonight. There is certain contamination in the atmosphere of Earth from various causes. If you do not surround yourselves by your own Sun Presence and Radiation of this Substance from the Sacred Fire, then you have no insulation or protection from the substance in the atmosphere that is thrown off by discordant conditions. So if you care to cooperate with this which I offer, it is for the establishment of an atmosphere about you of Cosmic Light Substance from Our Ascended Master Octave. It isn't just Universal Light Substance—It's the Substance from the Ascended Masters' Octave that is charged with Eternal Perfection, and naturally, that allows the Unfed Flame in your own Heart to expand more rapidly for your more victorious accomplishment in outer world activities, as well as the attainment of the Ascension.

I assure you, the Angelic Host will give you every Assistance in this capacity to help you attain the Ascension as you've called. And when mankind awakens enough by allowing the desire for that Perfection to fill the outer self, when the outer self is completely filled with that consuming desire for the Perfection of the "Mighty I AM Presence" in the Ascension, and the consuming desire to pour the Great Universal Cosmic Christ Love to Life, you will find the Angelic Host ever about you. I trust you will enter into this deeply and understand the opportunity that is yours and the Assistance I would so love to give by calling Groups of the Angels of the Violet Flame to abide with you for this greater accomplishment for the nation and the world. I hope I may have your cooperation. *(applause)* Thank you, Precious Ones. Won't you be seated, please, and just remain so.

Now at night when you go to sleep, you can ask for a Group of the Angelic Host to guard the body and the atmosphere about it while you go to the Temples of Light of the Sacred Fire to absorb what is there that you are going to require the next day. Then when you return to the body in the morning, don't hesitate to call for a Group of the Angels of the Violet Flame, the Violet Consuming Flame, to abide with you all that day wherever you go, and help you do that which needs to be done to hold the Victory and Protection of all that is constructive. If you will become aware of the Presence of the Angels of the Violet Consuming Flame, it will not be long till you might see Them. As you give Them ac-

May Da Camara 1946.

ceptance and are aware of Their Presence and
let Them expand Their Sacred Fire Love through
you each day, that will become an atmosphere
about you in which many people will sense the
Presence of those Angels and will much more
rapidly cooperate with you.

This will help you greatly to overcome your
problems. It will dissolve much obstruction and
delay in your pathway, and I assure you, it is a
very harmonious way of attaining success. After
all, I told you a long time ago that I was very
practical, didn't I? I have all through the years
(applause) Thank you so much!

You can have the Assistance of these Angel
Groups to hold about you Their Sacred Fire
Love and Strength with a Call first thing in the
morning that you do not feel exhaustion during
the day. If you can fill yourselves and your
worlds with the full feeling and acceptance of
the Sacred Fire in and around you expanding
the Perfection of Its Cosmic Christ Love through
you, the more you can become aware of the Flow
of that Sacred Fire from your Higher Mental
Body into you and out through you, the more
you will be aware of your insulation from the
pressure of the outer world. As you ask or invite

the Angels of the Violet Consuming Flame to pour Their Sacred Fire Love in and around you as a Sun Presence, the more will you find conditions wherever you abide prepared for you to help you accomplish successfully anything that is constructive. This removes much delay, much obstruction, and as time goes on It will remove all uncertainty in you as to the Victory of your accomplishment.

The reason I am doing this is because there are certain Groups of the Angels of the Violet Consuming Flame who, after a certain amount of Service to unascended beings—not only the atmosphere of Earth, but the Earth itself is purified—will take embodiment in this world; and I am looking forward, through this Activity, to enabling a certain Group to take on physical embodiment after the world itself is purified and the Golden Age has been well brought into outer existence. If you care to cooperate in this manner, the Groups of Violet Flame Angels whom I shall direct to assist you will be those whom, if you will love them, you may assist them in their embodiments after you are Ascended.

This is a great—you can call it reciprocity or Divine Justice or Balance or anything you please—

but the Great Cosmic Law of the Love of the
Sacred Fire, if mankind would only understand It
and use It, would bring such Illumination, such
Peace and such Happiness and such Victorious
Accomplishment that individuals would feel their
Mastery much more quickly, and not allow themselves to be caught in outer world conditions that
enslave them. If you do not master outer world
conditions, they will master you. You're either
Master or you're not, and I can positively assure
you that the Angels of the Violet Consuming
Flame are Master wherever They come! So They
do assure you of your Victory! They do give Protection! They do expand the Love of the Sacred
Fire in and around you and before you to make
your pathway easier and to establish the Command for Perfection.

So Blessed Ones, They might seem invisible
to you tonight, but everything that is in the visible world today was one day in the invisible;
and who of you can tell Me what is in the invisible now that will become visible to you before
too long? Everything is coming out of the invisible and into the visible, and if you would like
to have the Angels of the Violet Consuming
Flame become visible, I assure you, it is perfectly

possible. I am not talking in riddles, and I am not telling any fairy tales. I am offering you one of the most practical ways and means of living, and one of the most wonderful ways and means of drawing God's Perfection into a world whose shadows are seeking always to desecrate that which was God-created.

These Legions of the Angels of the Violet Consuming Flame can ever stand about you and will give much Assistance of which you will not be aware for some time to come. So if you want to start in tomorrow morning, I shall cooperate with you! *(applause)* Thank you so much, Precious Ones. When you awaken in the morning, if you will make your Call to your "Beloved Mighty I AM Presence" first, and to Me, for a Group of Violet Flame Angels to keep the Sacred Fire of Their Love in and around you for the entire day, let us experiment and see what you can have in a short time. And I hope you'll keep track of these—I mean, keep a record, at least mentally—of the days that you keep most consciously aware of the Angelic Host.

I assure you, *"I AM" Angel Bells* was not written by any accident. It is an Adoration and a Call to the Angelic Host for Their Presence with you, and if you will notice the lyrics, you are asked to join Their Legions! So if you make your Calls, Their Legions will join you, and we shall go forth together and do that which needs to be done. In the doing there will be only happiness, and your Mastery will be attained very much more comfortably and very much more quickly.

So I commend you to the Victory of the Angelic Host! May the Angels of the Violet Flame attend you tonight as you come to Me in the Violet Flame Temple. I hope you will remember the Music and the Love that will greet you there, and which you will absorb and bring back in the morning to bless you and all you contact. And so I trust that your greater Freedom will be very tangible in this cooperation which We wish to offer, which I know will bless you, and which will carry you forward with greater strength and give you greater Power of Victorious Accomplishment.

Thank you with all My Heart's Love! I call the Legions of the Angels of the Violet Consuming Flame to pour the Love of Their Sacred Fire ever about you until Its Freedom is a Sun Presence about you forever, and wherever you abide, you give It to others as the Angels of the Violet Consuming Flame are ready and willing to give It to you. Thank you with all My Heart.

CHAPTER X

BELOVED MIGHTY ASTREA

Santa Fe, New Mexico
April 30, 1962
Record CD 864

Blessed Beings of God's Heart, in the opportunity that lies ahead of you to cooperate with Us and draw into outer physical conditions whatever compels their Purification, you'll find coming in, through, and around you many ways and means of assistance that heretofore you have not experienced. It will give you many opportunities now to draw into outer physical conditions the Powers which We are directing to change the feeling of the people enough to make the intellect let go of the misinformation that has caused distress to Life, that causes people to do destructive things.

In all the Service We give to Life, We must work through the individual, except at certain Cosmic Moments when the Sacred Fire passes through the atmosphere of Earth and through the whole system for greater Purification, and the increasing of the vibratory action so that more Light expands through the whole system. But the rest of the time, whatever help We give, We must give through the people themselves.

Therefore as you associate with the people of the outer world through your radiation, your "Presence" and We can do many things without your saying a word; and sometimes the silence is very much more powerful than the spoken word. There is a proper time for each; but in all that you do, if you will try always to remember to call the Sun Presence of the Victory of Eternal Peace in and around yourself before you start in to handle a situation. That will give your "Presence" the stillness and control in the outer that will enable the right ideas to come through, and will enable It to pour forth the Harmony that will enable you to do the right thing at the right time and in the right way. Then as you ask to be enfolded in the Sun Presence of whatever Sacred Fire Love from the Ascended Masters' Octave will make you victorious in every condition of the outer world, then We can come to your assistance; and clothing the outer self in those

Activities of the Sacred Fire from the Ascended Masters' Octave that are Power without limit, It surrounds you with the Cosmic Vibratory Action from Our Octave that clothes whatever you are doing in the Protection you require to keep destructive forces from either intruding or interfering with you, or trying to destroy the good you are seeking to manifest.

Now My Legions of the Angels of the Flaming Sword are no figment of anybody's imagination, and I say to all destructive forces, they better not doubt Their existence in the Universe! A human being would be very unwise to deny the existence of the Great Cosmic Beings, the Legions of the Angels of the Flaming Sword, who as They move through the atmosphere of Earth, by the Flame from that Sword can consume in the atmosphere the frightful creations mankind has generated through hate, selfishness, violence and diabolical activities.

I wish you to understand something of what those Legions have rendered in the Service of the past. When that school of black magicians was broken up—and there were three hundred of them working against mankind at one time—I assure you, the Angels of the Flaming Sword were the Legions that came in and broke up the focus of those destructive activities that had been held for many centuries. It isn't wise to doubt the existence of Beings who have Power enough to undo mankind's destructive creation and who are wise enough to make no mistakes! Whenever you think of the Limitless Legions of the Angels of the Flaming Sword, know always They are Ascended Masters and Cosmic Beings who have been Ascended for a long time, and whose Power is absolutely Invincible and immediately Victorious!

So We would appreciate it greatly if you would ask, or send forth your Call in your Decrees, to fill your Nation with the Angels of the Flaming Sword, that They may go everywhere within your borders and consume completely, annihilate completely, every way and means by which the sinister force could stir up the people to do that which would produce the third episode of Washington's Vision. And this is the way They operate. Now I am speaking of the Legions of the Angels of the Flaming Sword. Wherever there is a vortex or an accumulation of energy being gathered by individuals who are determined to stir up trouble, wherever that force is being generated, the Angels of the Flaming Sword sweep in, and with that Sword of Flame consume that, and take the power out of the hands of those who are determined to destroy; for I assure you, They are very efficient! *(applause)* Thank you so much.

They can sweep into a condition and compel one destructive thing after another to collapse completely. Then the sinister force starts to build something else in its place. But these Great Beings are Master of manifestation! And because there has been generated hatred, race hatred, within the borders of the United States of America, the sinister force is using that race hatred—and all kinds of hate for any reason whatsoever in the feeling of the people—to be the pressure on the emotional bodies of those who are emotionally uncontrolled to stir them into violence simply to cause greater and greater destruction. It is the part of Wisdom at this time, which We are directing, to call these Legions of the Flaming Sword into every condition within your borders that creates or sustains the intention to create violence of any kind within your borders or against your people.

If you will remember this from tonight and call these Legions into every condition that you hear about or that you see trying to impose desecration upon the Nation or the people, We will set into action, at the Inner Level, certain Currents of the Cosmic Light Substance and certain Activities of the Sacred Fire that can go into the cities where these conditions are being generated, and keep consuming the discord that unfortunate individuals are trying to create in order to break loose slaughter and violence within your borders.

Now some of these groups openly admit that they simply hate certain portions of the population, so this is very necessary at this particular time in order to avoid the crisis which would give destructive forces the opportunity they want to do more damage. If you will remind yourselves frequently that all through the ages mankind has been reminded again and again, "Call unto Me and I will answer thee." That is the Greater Life in the Universe around this world that has offered help to mankind in conditions of this sort as they've happened down through the ages.

The outer intellect of mankind has been reminded repeatedly to call to the Great "God Presence" of Life for the help required to overcome the viciousness generated by mankind. So from tonight We are very definitely concentrating certain Activities of the Sacred Fire within every large city in this Nation. Now let Us prepare ahead of time and gather the momentum of Sacred Fire needed to prevent the slaughter intended. We can prevent that by your Call for Our Legions of the Angels of the Flaming Sword to move into every big city within this Nation and establish for all Eternity every Activity of the Sacred Fire that will forever prevent the hordes of evil and desecration from even getting started to produce the destruction they intend. And that's why I am here tonight! Those who minister with Me are already at work, or already in action, drawing in and around all conditions that are constructive these Activities of the Sacred Fire, and We will fan that, so to speak, until It spreads and expands and throws over destructive conditions intended the Power that shuts off their action until they are dissolved and consumed.

Please do not let the day go by that you don't demand the Great Central Sun's Cosmic Christ Blue Lightning Annihilation of all hate in all Life everywhere forever in this world! Your fierce demand for the Cosmic Law's Annihilation of that hate can come forth into this physical world and act in many channels with which you're not in touch, but which are generating hate that will unite the destructive conditions over the Nation that can produce disaster. If you call these forth also to annihilate everything that the atomic bombs have produced in the atmosphere of Earth, and all other destructive forces, those who govern the Powers of Nature and Forces of the Elements can set into action this Consuming Power and prevent that which otherwise will take place. You can't fool with the energy of Life! Nobody can without penalty!

So since there are those unfortunate individuals who have been caught in the whirlwind of hate generated sometimes many lifetimes; and since many of them have deliberate, intentional plans for desecration and destruction of anything that is decent, anything that's constructive, then there must come this greater Activity of the Sacred Fire to prevent and to offset that which has already gathered within the borders of this Nation. Sometime each day, if you will demand the Great Central Sun's Cosmic Christ Blue Lightning Purifying Annihilation of all hate in every big city within your borders, and all hate in those who want only to destroy or desecrate, then that can be intensified every day. And We can produce that much more rapidly than the destructive forces can gather the power to do what they want to do in open violence!

So don't waste time criticizing, blaming, condemning anybody or anything. Just keep pouring on the Great Central Sun's Cosmic Christ Blue Lightning Purity that forever prevents hate in any of the big cities of your Nation, then everywhere throughout the Nation. Hate is what feeds the feeling of mankind, especially individuals who are uncontrolled emotionally. If it touches that uncontrolled energy, well, it qualifies it, that's all! But the Sacred Fire Purity from the Great Central Sun which We direct and which the Angels of the Flaming Sword direct, that Purity can go into the energy that has already been qualified with hate, and that Sacred Fire can consume the hate, and the energy thus purified can be used to protect that which is constructive and act as a barrier to those who want to enter in to release that destruction.

So this is a very Wise, Powerful, Cosmic Way to trap the enemy until the enemy is helpless. When you make the conscious effort to call to Life, the "Beloved I AM Presence" and the Ascended

Host—the Angels of the Flaming Sword—to blaze into a condition the Great Central Sun's Eternal Cosmic Christ Blue Lightning Purity, that Sacred Fire going into the energy that's been qualified with hate will consume the hate. Then It enters into that energy and qualifies it with Its own Sacred Fire and holds it for constructive activity and Protection for all that is of the Light. This is the way you take the wind out of the sails of the enemy; and more than that, it's a raising activity to the Life Streams who generated that hate, because when you draw that energy off and consume the hate, that energy belonging to that Life Stream, when purified and raised into a higher vibratory action, must raise that Life Stream to greater constructive activity.

So you have a threefold Blessing in this Call. Even from the standpoint of selfishness, it's the wisest thing to do to obey the Law—and I'm speaking of the Divine Law of Eternal Mastery. Blessed Ones, when conditions that come to your attention every day in the outer world reveal that hatred and criticism and condemnation are being generated here and there and everywhere, it is simply gathering a storm cloud of hate. If every day you will demand all the hatred generated in

the Nation, the feeling of the people, be wiped
out of the Universe *every day,* you'll find the
Light will accumulate, and the destructive forces
will not be able to gather the Power to do what
they want to do. We have many ways and means
of offsetting the plans of the sinister force. By
taking away from them the energy by which
they do their damage, they will be unable to
accomplish their destructive ends.

I am hoping that you will experiment with
this and enjoy It so much that you will become
experts in calling It into action! Then you do not
need to argue. You can, by the Power of the
Great Great Silence, you can offset destructive
forces until they are completely removed from
this world. This is part of the Power of the Great
Great Silence. This is an overwhelming Action
of the Sacred Fire. I assure you, It is the
Wisdom and the Intelligence of the "Mighty
I AM Presence" and the Ascended Host, and It
will enable you to be victorious without that
sense of personal fight or antagonism or battle
between individuals.

If people would only learn to be silent and call
the Sacred Fire Silence into the condition with
the demand that It annihilate everything destruc-

tive, you would find the "Mighty I AM Presence" of each Life Stream or the Assisting Masters would handle the conditions around you without drawing you into a vortex of destructive activity because you are trying to raise the condition out of the control of destructive forces. So Blessed Ones, It is greater Protection to you all, and It is the action of the Prevention Flame.

If you call forth the Prevention Flame from the Great Great Silence to move into every big city in this Nation and prevent the hate that enables destructive forces to act, It will bless you. It'll charge you with Its Power, and the very Radiation around you will repel it from your own activities until the Nation is completely purified. So It is a very practical application of the energy of Life. If you particularly will do this each day in each large city so that the accumulation of the people, as they generate discord in outer activities, that accumulation—a certain amount of destructive feeling—is wiped out of existence every day; then it doesn't reach the place of a storm cloud. Then it doesn't burst back upon the people as revolution or riots and all that sort of thing.

Your public servants have been sacrificed to much of this hated, and they have done the best they could to guard against it. The forces are infiltrated into the feeling of the people, and you must stay insulated against that hatred, and you must stay free from connection with the outer physical activities. And you can do this by making this Call. If you ask for the Great Central Sun's Cosmic Christ Blue Lightning Purity to sweep into every big city within this Land, and every day consume all the hatred that has been generated in each city, We can draw that off, and the Power of the Great Central Sun Magnet will raise what is constructive within each city into more Power and Activity of the Light; and therefore release from within each Life Stream an expansion of the Light that holds Protection and Victory for that which is constructive.

So It has a double Blessing to you all, and to the Nation, and to the world. I hope with all My Heart you will set into action with this. And don't be off guard! When these forces do diabolical things, don't argue, don't stop to have any opinions. Just move into action and demand whatever Sacred Fire Purity and Blue Lightning Power from the Great Central Sun is necessary to consume all hate, and to prevent anything and everything that produces violence within your borders!

We will help in every way possible! We will use all the Power at Our Command and do everything the Cosmic Law permits as you take the Scepter of Power and move into outer conditions by your authority and use of the Great Central Sun's Cosmic Christ Blue Lightning Purity. Charge It into every bit of energy where impurity has gone forth, and let Us see what We can do as quickly as possible in the next thirty days. I will give you every Assistance! Our Legions are forever ready, and these Activities can act on the instant. If you will make an effort to do this, We will appreciate it greatly; for it will enable Us to do more. If you do a certain amount of this yourselves, it will enable Us to use more Power than otherwise could come at this time within your borders.

So I commend you to the Victory We want you to have! We know you have the power to make the Call; the Cosmic Law is ready to act; the Sacred Fire is ever available, and We stand ready to amplify It without limit until the complete removal of the sinister force from the Earth puts an end to the frightful discord that has been generated here. We are ever with you and will do everything possible to amplify that which you send forth. We absolutely demand your Victory, your Protection, and your Invincible Freedom from the desecration intended. Our Legions of the Angels of the Flaming Sword can ever stand around you, and with that Sword in constant motion in every direction, can enfold you in Its Presence. And I assure you, no human creation will ever pass through that Flame! We offer this to every one of you for your Protection until the Victory of the world is complete for Eternity. Thank you with all Our Love!

CHAPTER XI

BELOVED ANGEL DEVA OF THE
JADE TEMPLE

Santa Fe, New Mexico
May 4, 1962
Record CD 868

Beloved Ones of the Precious Saint Germain's Family, I have come tonight to bring you an Explanation of some of the things the Angelic Host do to help mankind to protect that which is constructive, and to bring the Illumination that must one day take Its Dominion through all Life in this world. I wish you to understand that from Our Great Temples of the Sacred Fire there is streaming forth—not only into the atmosphere of Earth, but coming right into the structure of Earth itself—Great Cosmic Light Rays and Great Cosmic Streams of the Sacred Fire, concentrated at certain places in the structure of the Earth where those Mighty Outpourings continue to flow, to expand, to purify, and to harmonize.

The mass of mankind does not understand this. You have no idea how many of those Mighty Cosmic Activities are anchored into the physical structure of the Earth itself to enable mankind to continue to live here and make conscious effort to attain the Ascension. Mankind knows very little about the Great Cosmic Divine Plan and Law of the Life that creates a planet, brings forth the Powers of Nature upon it, and provides conditions here in which mankind may embody. Now the Ascended Masters and Cosmic Beings, from Their Great Temples of the Sacred Fire which are Their Homes and Focus of Activity throughout Creation, in those Temples of the Sacred Fire there is concentrated the Cosmic Power of the special Activities which They are directing to the Earth or to this system of worlds.

My Service from the Jade Temple is to intensify the Activity of Purification, because the Jade Temple and the Jade that is placed in the structure of Earth, as it grows through the Powers of Nature, is an Eternally Pure Substance. Jade will not take on the magnetic radiation of impurity from mankind's feeling. Therefore We can call forth through that a continual Flow of Our Purifying Power, the Light Rays and Cosmic Light Substance that continually radiate into outer world conditions Our Eternal Purity. If it were not so—that these Great Streams of Cosmic Light Substance and the Sacred Fire—if They were not placed within the structure of Earth itself; if We were to suddenly withdraw that, everything would return to the unmanifest.

This is the Divine Plan and Action of Life, the Cosmic Life that surrounds this system of worlds by which manifestation is drawn into existence, is sustained, and goes on expanding its activity while mankind takes embodiment here to fulfill the Divine Plan of the Ascension. From the Ascended Masters' Temples of the various Activities of the Jewels of the Sacred Fire and of the Cosmic Light—the condensation of that Cosmic Light Substance—these are the Mighty, Sustaining Activities of the Cosmic Light that is the Great Manifesting Substance by which a world exists.

So when We come from time to time and pour Our Radiation to you and intensify Our Outpouring through the Substance We have created here and placed within the Powers of Nature, it is that a certain proportion of Purity, Eternal Purity, flows continually here in this world in order to sustain it; and in order to have constructive activities in which mankind can function to learn the Great Laws of the Universe, to draw forth the Great Power of Life's Creative Activities, and to gain the experience here by which each individual becomes an Ascended Being.

So when you think of Us, when you hear of the Angel Devas, remember always, We are the Cosmic Life's Activity that is constantly creating that which is constructive and pouring It forth into the Earth, the structure of Earth, and into the people, to fulfill the Great Divine Plan. Whenever you care to accept or call forth individually into yourselves or your affairs the Purifying Power that We are giving and that comes under Our Direction, you may have an individualized Stream of each of these Great Activities anchored in and around you—so long as you accept It, call for It, love It, give It recognition, and let Us have a chance to expand It in, through, and around you. So Our Gift is continually blessing Life and raising It into something greater and more magnificent in Its Perfection from Our Octave and Its ever-increasing Happiness to Life in this world.

There are great Departments in the Activities
of Nature over which We preside, and through
which We are definitely constructing magnificent Beauty and Perfection for the future of this
world. You can just as well have more of Our
Perfection—and Beauty and Perfection, Beauty
and Sacred Fire Love that belongs into the use
of mankind; so long as the Divine Plan is being
fulfilled, and so long as the desire in life is to do
that which is constructive. The Great Cosmic
Law of Life is so wonderful, Beloved Ones,
because the moment any desire within an individual is constructive, the Greater Life surrounding the individual will always make every
effort to fulfill every constructive desire, give all
cooperation, and let It manifest the Divine Plan
revealed so It may lift Life everywhere into
greater Perfection and Happiness.

Now the Angelic Host are the Custodians of
Mighty Gifts in the use of the Powers of Life. We
not only are Their Guarding Presence; We are
the Givers of these Magnificent Creations that
exist in Our Temples of the Sacred Fire—or the
Jewels—all of which are concerned with the pouring forth of the Powers and the Perfection and the
Activity of the Sacred Fire and the Cosmic Light.

As We give that to this world or to the system, the Power in Our Temples of the Sacred Fire ever expands the Focus of the Sacred Fire there till each one of Our Temples one day becomes a Sun. And so can it be with you in this world— your home, your business activities, your outer personal accomplishments. As you call forth this greater Perfection from Our Octave, your world becomes the Focus of a Sun Presence of the Sacred Fire of Our Love, Our Life, Our Substance, Our Purity—therefore Our Mastery and Our Perfection.

Every particle of life can have every Assistance from all the Greater Life whenever the desire is to produce Perfection, regardless of what channel that is in. You take the mechanical world for instance. When an individual who has great genius in mechanical activities, and is what you call a precision mechanic; whenever there is the desire within Life to produce Perfection in manifestation, there will always come some Being from the Angelic Host to give that Assistance, because it brings more Light into the manifested substance of this world and its atmosphere, and therefore into the Life Stream of individuals.

That desire within you or within any part of Life to produce Perfection is an Expansion of the Light from the Higher Mental Body of the "Mighty I AM Presence." Every desire to produce Perfection is an Expansion of the Light. Since We live to bring the Greater Light everywhere into manifestation, then We give every Assistance wherever the Light begins to be revealed at the Inner Level. This is how We see the progress that mankind is making. This is how We know individuals are holding to the constructive way of life and are channels through which We can pour forth more Perfection, because at the Inner Level there flows—wherever the constructive desire is within the Life Stream, the outer self—it always manifests a Light.

So when We see at the Inner Level, as We look over all mankind, a Light shining brighter here or there or somewhere else, one or more of the Angelic Host will always come, observe that Light, observe that individual, and try to give every possible help to keep that Light protected and expanding. This is a very wonderful Activity of Life, and if mankind knew more about the Angelic Host, individuals could have very much greater Help in all outer constructive activity.

And We are here to give that to those who want It! *(applause)* Thank you so much, Precious Ones. Won't you be seated, please, and just remain so.

Now Our Temples of the Sacred Fire are—each one—a Powerhouse, a Focus of Cosmic Power of Our Life, of Our Desires of the past which have drawn forth these Magnificent Cosmic Activities of the Sacred Fire to create Perfection, and then send It forth into the planets of the system to ever expand the Light and the Greater Perfection. So the Law of Our World is to give! The only way the Light can expand is for someone to pour more of the life of the individual and the love within that life that is luminosity. That's what illumines the Universe. You, as individuals, can be a Light in the consciousness of mankind. You can be a Light in the feeling of mankind to produce Peace. Everything in your life can be an outpouring of luminosity to help you move forward and produce the greater Perfection that is greater Freedom for all.

Do you remember the Beloved Saint Germain saying it is as easy to illumine the atmosphere as it is for you to touch a switch on the wall and turn on the electricity in the lights! When you understand the Oneness of the Great Universal

Light—which We sometimes speak of as the Cosmic Light—when you understand that that is Eternal Light, then It is there! And the only thing that keeps It from flooding here without limit is the vibratory action around human beings of feeling and thought and action that is the slower rate of vibration, and that forms the veil between your outer activity and Our Outer Activity. That's in the atmosphere of Earth. It is in the aura of individuals.

Now since everything that the Angelic Host does for mankind is to bring only Purity into manifestation—because We can't produce anything else—then if mankind is to have relief from the destruction that impurity has created, then individuals are going to have to know of Our Presence. The outer activity of mankind is going to have to cooperate with Us if We are going to pour the Purity of Our Sacred Fire into the conditions to hold that which is constructive to serve the people while they make effort to attain the Ascension. So it matters not what is in manifestation in this world, whatever is constructive is guarded by, sustained by, and forever enfolded in some Activity from the Angelic Host. Only as individuals understand this, cooperate with it, and learn the Law of its manifestation, can We make each one in the outer an outpost of Ourselves, that locally you may have Our Assistance, so long as your outer activity is to bring more Illumination—explanation—to the life of mankind embodied here.

So the condition on which We can flood everything good to you is that you are concerned with the pouring forth of everything good to the rest of Life, so that you are a channel for Our Greater Good to come in and bless you. You are an open door and a channel for your greater Good to flow onto those you contact. This is a continual giving of the Greater Light from Our Octave, the Greater Activities of the Sacred Fire, and the Greater Power by which the life in individuals is raised to the place where the individual can make conscious effort to the Ascension.

While there is very great enjoyment in using all the Powers of your own individual Life Streams in your outer activities, yet the most necessary and the greatest Accomplishment that individuals can attain is to consciously understand the Ascension is the purpose of physical embodiment. To make effort towards the Ascension is not only opening the Door to Eternal Happiness, but it is the Attainment of those Powers that make you Master over the manifestations in this world and other worlds.

The Mighty Outpouring from the Jade Temple is also the Direction into the substance of this world—and through the consciousness of man-kind—of a certain vibratory action of certain colors. These colors have definite effect within the feeling world and the consciousness of the individuals to whom they are directed. Since the balance is required in the physical octave to keep you insulated against destructive forces, the most necessary thing for mankind to understand is to call forth into the outer self the Activities of the Sacred Fire of Eternal Purity. So when We've sent forth a Light Ray of a certain color to pour forth into a locality or an individual or some activity of mankind, that which We give is to establish permanently the vibratory action of that particular quality and constructive activity that strengthens everything within the Life Stream that enables Perfection to manifest.

So it is the Light We give, the Love We give. The Sacred Fire We give is the Sustaining Life from Our Temples of the Sacred Fire to the bodies of mankind, to the activities of the individual; to establish in this world the greater Blessing and Perfection and Power to produce Perfection from Our World that gradually closes the door against mankind's, not only mistakes of the past, but mankind's creation of that which is not perfect. So the Temples of the Sacred Fire in the Electronic Belts around the Physical Sun and the Great Central Sun are the individual Powerhouses, so to speak, of the Ascended Masters or Cosmic Beings who have taken the responsibility of directing to this world what is needed here to shut off mankind's further creation of destruction, and to begin to build here that which will be the Permanent Blessing of the future.

If you want to understand something of what the Activities from the Jade Temple are, then ask your "Beloved I AM Presence" and Me to charge you with what We know that Activity of Life can bring to this world to help you, and to understand what the Greater Life has placed in Our Temple of Jade to bring forth here Its Blessings of Eternal, Expanding Power and Perfection. Blessed Ones, these Gifts are in the Universe! They are the natural Action of Life! They are as free as the air you breathe, but They come un-

der Obedience to the Law. Those who will place
their attention upon Our Activities, ask for the
Illumination, and cooperate by keeping the Harmony and Purity in the outer self, can open the
floodgates to supply that you could not use in a
thousand years!

We are part of the supply of the Blessings to
Life in this world! We are part of the Divine Plan
by which Blessings are supplied to the people of
this world. These greater Perfect Activities and
the Blessings of the greater Perfection in Our
Temples of the Sacred Fire are provided by Life
to arouse mankind to a desire to do something
greater and better, and to understand more of
the Infinite Universe by which individuals are
surrounded. You may have everything We
have—and know all We know—when you maintain Purity in the outer, and Obedience, which
is Harmony, use your Violet Flame and send
the Adoration of Love to your "Presence" and
to Us. Your Mighty Saint Germain told you
there is no barrier anywhere in the Universe to
Pure Divine Love, because It is the Sacred Fire
that can burn Its Way through everything, and
produce the Perfection that ever transmutes everything in existence into something greater and

better—that releases more Happiness and more Freedom to life wherever It is called into existence.

So Beloved Ones, the Angelic Host's Blessing to mankind is without limit. I could go on almost indefinitely and describe some of the Greater Activities of the Angelic Host, but if you will use what We have given, then as you are ready for more, We will give more! But there is no use in giving more than you can understand or use at the present time. And you only know as much as you are! You do not know in your feeling anything except what you are. So if you are to learn what Our Magnificent Blessings to Life are, then you must become Them. Then you understand Them, and They automatically will teach you inside of yourselves what the Powers are within those Blessings when you use Them. Mankind may have intellectual knowledge, but people do not know even intellectually the real Truth of Existence unless the outer self becomes the Flame of Its Perfection. Therefore it is necessary to purify the feeling! It is necessary to purify the substance of the body, and purify the atmosphere around it in order that We may teach you and make you know what Our Greater Life can do in you, and through you, and around you—for you—by your own use of the Powers of Our Life which We convey to you through the Sacred Fire and the Cosmic Light Substance and Our Love.

These things are the natural, Divine Way of Life to manage things in this world and thus avoid the problems and the limitations which are nothing on Earth but mankind's lack of understanding of the Great Law of the Sacred Fire, the Cosmic Light, and the Love from the Heart of Creation. That's why it is necessary that there must come more Conscious Cooperation between mankind and the Angelic Host. It's the only way Perfection and improvement can come into this world, because It's the Divine Plan of Creation from the Great Central Sun to the Electrons and the atoms out of which manifestation is composed. This is the Great Supply House of the Universe, and there isn't a thing your life could desire, so long as it be constructive, that Our Life could not supply. So there is no reason in Heaven or Earth that you shouldn't reach up to the Highest, receive Our Help, and create the most Magnificent Perfection in this world—not for your own, to feed your own egotism, not at all—but to give you the Joy of the use of the Master Powers of Life.

You can only use Them as you produce Manifestation in this world by Their Use that will bless some other part of Life. So the supreme secret is the blessing of Life! Don't be concerned whether the other part of Life that you are pouring the blessing to appreciates it or not! What do you care? If We waited for mankind's appreciation *(laughter)* well, We waited a long time as it is, but We'd wait a lot longer—much longer! Your expansion of your Light and your Powers of your Life's Perfection can only come into existence by your use of Them, and your use of Them must bless the rest of the Life around you. If you pour that Blessing out, the very Life from Our Octave and from the Higher Mental Body of each one's Life Stream will amplify that good that you produce, and in Its Expansion, It will come back and bless you.

So you cannot lose by using these Greater Powers of Life's Perfection! Therefore I offer you tonight the Gifts that I can give from the Jade Temple. Then one day, there will come into this world a Focus of a Special Activity that is contained within Jade; and that is established for centuries to pour forth Its constant, Purifying Radiation to sustain that which is constructive and to ever create greater Blessings and more magnificent civilizations that will bless the rest of Life and make the Pathway to the Ascension easier, happier, more invincible, and always Victorious. These are the Gifts that We can give. This is Our Service to Life. So if you care to accompany Us to some of Our Heights of Magnificent Activity, We can reveal to you this Greater Perfection and Joy of Life. And then if you will let Us pour Our Greater Purity through you to create more Beauty and Perfection in this world, It can only bring you greater Happiness and a greater Raising Activity to lift you to your Ascension.

So Blessed Ones, go on, and call into the physical world the magnificent Powers of the Angelic Host that reveal to mankind what all individuals can have; as they understand to co-operate with the Greater Life and the Greater Blessings they can use is to bring those Blessings here in the physical world for your greater Perfection, your greater harmony and your greater ease in attaining the Ascension. So go forward, and if you care to call to Me, I will have very Great Joy illumining you and showing you some of the things I can do for Life, and revealing to you some of the Blessings in the Jade Temple that one day will fill this world, too, with the same Happiness and Beauty and Perfection We have there. I hope you will enjoy the greater use of these Blessings that We want you to have, that you may fill your world with the same Great Happiness that fills Ours. And then you will be so busy expanding that Happiness, you will have forgotten forever that you ever went through the experience of the shadows in which suffering was experienced by mankind. As your Greater Creative Activity goes forward like Ours, you will forget the distress and the limitations through which you have passed, and you will not look back, because the Perfection of the future will draw you on into itself, and you will forever leave the shadows behind.

Thank you with all My Heart.

CHAPTER XII

BELOVED LADY MASTER NADA

Shasta Springs, California
September 18, 1962
Record CD 943; Casssette 60016

Beloved Ones of My Heart, tonight I trust I may bring to you the Comprehending Consciousness of what Our Love and Mercy means to Life, that you may understand while yet unascended something of the Ascended Masters' Way to help Life wherever you abide to awaken from the shadows, to turn Godward, and to behold the Mastery which each one may become, and must someday manifest in the Great Cosmic Activities of Life's Perfection everywhere.

In calling into outer physical conditions these Cosmic Activities of the Violet Consuming Flame and the Unfed Flame, the Sevenfold Flame of the Seven Mighty Elohim—all Activities of the Sacred Fire—into the physical octave, I wish you to un-

derstand that there is an Inner Action of the
Cosmic Law of Love, Forgiveness, and Mercy
that can bring to you very, very great Help to
yourselves individually when you call It forth for
the release of Life everywhere from the human
creation of the past and present.

Many times your loved ones are caught in
conditions from which at the present time they
do not seem to be able to extricate themselves.
But I wish you to understand how the Cosmic
Law of Love and Mercy, in the use of the Violet
Consuming Flame in your Calls to Us can bring
Assistance. Many times there are those in the
outer world who are doing things that are wrong;
the mass accumulation imposes very great injus-
tice upon Life. You see it acting in families, in
business, in politics, in the nations and govern-
ments of the world, and also in activities that
affect all mankind at the same time. It also acts
through the Powers of Nature and Forces of the
Elements.

This is what has been done many times down
through the centuries by those who were willing
to give to Life some tremendous service to cut
free many Life Streams from a certain amount of
human creation; that the Great Law of Love and

Mercy, Forgiveness and Balance would take away from the loved one much of the accumulation, and enable that loved one to go forward and serve the Light in the future. This is an Activity of Divine Justice. It's an Activity of Love and Mercy and Balance to Life. Therefore We bring it to your attention tonight that you may render certain service in outer physical conditions that will not only enable the Great Law of Balance to flow in and around you for your own personal freedom, but will flow to your loved ones and consume some of their human creation—strengthen the Light by the enfolding love which you send, which enables the individual to hold the attention upon the constructive way of life long enough to decide to turn and serve that constructive way of life permanently.

Now you can render this service not only to unascended beings, but to those who are resting between embodiments. If they are your loved ones and have not had this knowledge of the "Mighty I AM Presence," by this your service to Life Streams in this world that are caught in the shadows, and by your Demand for the annihilation of whatever human creation enslaves them, you can say to your "Beloved I AM Presence" and the Ascended Host and the Great Cosmic Law of the Violet Consuming Flame: "In Thy Great Love, Mercy, and Forgiveness to Life, I ask for whatever Dispensation and Release of the Violet Consuming Flame is necessary to annihilate that human creation which enslaves that Life Stream"—or many of them if you're working with groups. "I ask this Mercy to Life, and I ask at the same time the Great Cosmic Law of the Violet Consuming Flame's Love, Mercy, and Forgiveness to Life to my loved ones who as yet seem not to be serving the Light."

Let this go forth to the loved ones embodied. Let It go forth to the loved ones who are out of physical embodiment at this time. This renders tremendous service, Beloved Ones! It consumes a great deal of the hardness in people's feeling which makes them do wrong. I bring It to your attention tonight because It's very much required, very much needed in the physical world. It was this Great Love, Mercy, and Forgiveness to Life which the Blessed Quan Yin had become to the world down through the centuries. And that is why She said, "I will not enter Heaven until there are no more in the distress of the physical world." This is a tremendous Service to Life.

There are certain Groups of the Ascended Host who concentrate on this. The Angelic Host particularly have a Group of those whose Concentrated Action is the Sacred Fire's Purity in Love, Forgiveness, and Mercy to set Life free from enough human creation to let the individual awaken—and the Higher Mental Body of that Life Stream strengthen the Light in the outer self, to make the outer intellectual consciousness, and the emotional body, let the desire from the Heart Flame of the individual have Its Dominion, and turn the outer self to the Light with the desire to give obedience, and fulfill the Requirements of the Cosmic Law to the Freedom of the Ascension. So it is a mighty service to Life, Beloved Ones, to release individuals from the hardness of human feelings which but enslave them to greater and greater destruction.

I think you've heard many times the Messenger tell of the experience of the Blessed Master Kuthumi when his Life Stream was at the testing time, and he stood, as it were, upon a knife edge of two forces. Just a breath could have thrown him into the destructive activities, and just a wave, one wave of Love, drew him into the Service of the Light. And that experience was a

tremendous thing. He said in the hour when he
of his own Free Will had to make his choice as
to whom he was going to serve—which activity
of Life—He said an uncle whom he loved very
greatly and who loved him very greatly, just one
wave of the love from that uncle who was
thinking about him made him decide to go the
constructive way of life. That's why no one can
approximate how great is the Power that can be
released; and how great will the love render its
Service to Life when We pour forth the Cosmic
Call for Sacred Fire Love to strengthen the Life
Streams of those whom we love, be they embodied or disembodied—strengthen those Life
Streams by Our Love—strong enough to make
them desire to go the constructive way of life.

So no earnest effort is lost! Not one wave of
sincere, unselfish Love—the Sacred Fire Love of
the Cosmic Christ—not one wave can go out that
does not eternally bless Life. And that's what the
world needs since the world is taking its Initiation
in Love. Surely those of you who understand this
Law, I'm quite sure you will see what service you
can render to many Life Streams—whom you do
not know—may be struggling with all they are
and have to try to hold to the constructive way

of life; but the pressure of the mass accumulation of mankind's discord is so heavy upon them because of their own accumulation and desires of the past, that the struggle is one of life and death, the struggle to either go to the Light or the struggle that allows the destructive force to swallow up the individual into the destructive activities that sooner or later destroy everything. You cannot approximate the Power in just one wave of feeling of love to Life that asks for Love, Forgiveness, and Mercy to strengthen every Life Stream and enfold every Life Stream in that Sacred Fire Power of All-purifying Love that holds it to the constructive way of life in the hour of its greatest trial.

This is the Love, Forgiveness, and Mercy which the Beloved Master Jesus taught, and which every Ascended Master not only has taught, but is to Life at all times. You do not know, and will not know until your Ascension, in some of your own experiences when you almost swung to destructive forces. You do not know whose wave of Love was the magnetic pull that drew you onto the constructive way of life. So don't ever presume to pass judgment on anyone else. You do not know how much Assistance the Love of one or more of the Ascended Host, and many times the sincere, unselfish love of some of your family, your relatives or your friends might have been the delicate touch, and just the small amount of energy needed to hold you to the constructive way of life when you were wavering and the destructive forces were pulling you the other way.

So from tonight I hope I may be of Service in this direction, because it is one of the great Avenues of Service which We render in Our Assistance to mankind through the Powers of Healing. *(applause)* Thank you so much. The Beloved Mary all through the ages has been concerned with, and one of Her principal Activities to bless the people of this world, is that of bringing the Purity that always produces Healing. The Beloved Meta also is one of those who is Authority over the healing of all mankind, as is Beloved Mary, the Great Lord the Maha Chohan, Myself, the Beloved Quan Yin, and Legions of the Healing Angels.

Therefore, there are great Groups of the Angelic Host who are concerned just with pouring in and around human beings the Sacred Fire's Power Flame to make individuals feel more kindly to Life and more kindly to those who sometimes injure them. This Love, Forgiveness, and Mercy to Life must come, My Beloved Ones, because It is part of the Sacred Fire's Consuming Activity to consume the shadows and the substance which hate always creates and densifies and concentrates in and around individuals, until they will not let the constructive impulses of life have dominion through the outer self. The great Healing Activities of the whole world come under the Direction of the Great Lord the Maha Chohan and Legions of the Angelic Host, Ascended Beings who have chosen to concentrate Their Service to Life into the channels of Healing to bring Purification there which heals mankind permanently.

Therefore when you begin with the Great Central Sun's Cosmic Power and Sun Presence of the Sacred Fire's Healing Flame of Love, Forgiveness, and Mercy, as you maintain this by Conscious Command—that It go forth and consume all substance and all disease and all feeling that holds mankind bound in the destructive conditions of ill health and poverty and distress of every kind—do not fail, if you need this Assistance yourselves, or if you need and desire to

call It forth into outer physical conditions; not
only in healing channels but in many activities
of mankind where Love, Mercy, and Forgiveness
are needed in the physical octave of Life, to sal-
vage one Life Stream after another, and take it
out of the clutches of the destructive forces that
have sought to desecrate it and destroy it.

The need of this world for Love, Forgiveness,
and Mercy is very grave; and permanent Peace
cannot come to the Earth until this Love, Mercy,
and Forgiveness has entered in. This Sacred Fire
Purifying Love must come into the energy of
the emotional body of every individual if there
is to be enough Light in the physical world to
strengthen the constructive impulses in individuals to hold Peace. All the turmoil that is in
the various parts of the world tonight is the generation of discord—discordant feeling not only
just over the last few years; the mass accumulation has been gathering since the sinking of
Atlantis, which is fourteen thousand years ago.
This is a mass accumulation of mankind's hard
feeling.

So from tonight, whenever you see things that
are wrong in the outer world, just call the Great
Central Sun's Cosmic Legions of the Angelic

Host's Sacred Fire Consuming Love, Forgiveness, and Mercy that goes directly into the emotional body, into the feeling world of individuals and all Life, even into the animal life, and forces the consuming! This Cosmic Flame of Sacred Fire Love, Forgiveness, and Mercy to Life, entering into the energy of the feeling world, goes into it and consumes the hard feeling.

Now We enter into the use of the Law of Forgiveness. And My Dear Ones, you not only must forgive mankind's miscreation of this world, you must forgive your own. Who else can forgive it? Who else can give you the Violet Consuming Flame to act within yourselves but your own "Beloved I AM Presence" and the Ascended Host! Mankind cannot do it. Therefore, if you wish to become some of the Legions of Love—of the Sacred Fire's Love, Forgiveness, and Mercy to Life—We can move you into certain conditions, and while you are occupied with something that's constructive, there can flood forth in and around you Great Oceans, if need be, of the Sacred Fire from Our Octave, from Our Great Temples of the Sacred Fire, and from the Physical Sun and the Great Central Sun. There can flow Great Streams, Great Oceans of the Sacred Fire's Puri-

fying Love, Forgiveness, and Mercy to Life that
will soften the feeling of masses of the people,
and will consume the pressure upon the emotional bodies of the people to the point where
there can be released the desire from the Heart
to go forward and hold to that which is constructive.

This is the reason the Mighty Saint Germain
said that in this immediate activity of the present
century, as more of this Violet Consuming Flame
comes into outer world activities, many Life
Streams whom you thought could not and would
not turn to the Light at this time—because of the
accumulation of discord of the past—many of
those Life Streams will awaken and suddenly
decide to do the constructive thing, and will
surprise themselves and others also! So you never
can tell except through the Assistance of an
Ascended Being what is in the Causal Body of
the individual which suddenly can release the
Strength of Its Light into the outer self to turn
that one away from the clutches of destructive
conditions.

The Mighty Saint Germain told these Messengers some years ago that in dealing with
individuals—when from the outer self it seemed

the individual would not do right—He has given
opportunity again and again and again to help
the individual do right until He has exhausted
the opportunities for the individual to turn back
to the constructive way of life, and receive the
added Strength of the Light from the Causal
Body, and draw It into outer physical conditions
to balance the Life Stream, and make it strong
enough to go forward on the constructive way of
life. This is the way We balance forces from the
Inner Level, and no one can tell except an Ascended Being how much Light is in the Causal
Body. But every wave of Love, Pure Christ Love,
that you send to any part of Life is the Release
of the Sacred Fire and Cosmic Christ Substance
of Eternal Light, because Pure Christ Love is
Immortal. It is the Immortal Flame of your own
"Beloved I AM Presence" and the Ascended
Host.

Therefore when you call this forth into outer
conditions to force mankind to awaken and turn
away from the destructive forces that seek to
engulf them, you may render service, My Dear
Ones, that will bless thousands of Life Streams
for all centuries to come! If you care to join Us
in this Call to draw into physical conditions

quickly whatever Sacred Fire Power of the All-purifying Love of Cosmic Christ Control is necessary to strengthen the Life Streams of all who are constructive within this Nation, and then throughout the world; so that wherever possible the Light in the Life Stream expands Its Assistance to the rest of Life, and in that Expansion begins Its Pathway of Freedom to the Ascension. I know of nothing that is more required in the world tonight than Great Oceans of the Central Sun's Violet Flame's Love, Forgiveness, and Mercy to Life, to make every wave of Love that you send forth the Cosmic Christ Sacred Fire Love, Forgiveness, and Mercy that compels individuals to turn away from destructive conditions. And this is part of your Prevention Flame. It is the Love, Forgiveness, and Mercy which every Ascended Master must pour forth to Life if anyone is to gain the Ascension.

So I trust It will become for you such a Power of accomplishment that your loved ones, who perhaps are not doing the right thing at this time, can be awakened and taken out of the clutches of the hordes of evil that otherwise would try either to delay their Ascension or destroy their opportunities in this embodiment. It is a tremendous Service to give to Life. I know of nothing more important to hold control of the feeling of the people of the Nation than this Great Central Sun's Sacred Fire Power Flame of Love, Forgiveness, and Mercy that strengthens every Life Stream with the Light which compels it to turn Godward at this time and receive the Help that cuts away the destructive forces of the mass accumulation of mankind.

So if We may have your cooperation and your joining with Us as part of the Legions of the Angels of Love and Mercy and Forgiveness, the Angels of the Sacred Fire's Healing Purity to the Earth, Blessed Ones, you could not remain in distress. This would mean the healing of your bodies, the healing of the minds of the people, the healing of your affairs, the healing of the hate of nations. It is very much needed at this time, and We do hope you will reach up and use this Power which We are so glad to concentrate into your outer use if you wish to render this Service. *(applause)* Thank you so much, Precious Ones. Won't you be seated, please, and just remain so.

Everyone who has come to set mankind Free has reached the Momentum in the use of this

Power which has always been the enfolding
Sun Presence that rendered that Service of Illumination to mankind by the Love, Forgiveness,
and Mercy of the Sacred Fire. Now this does not
mean that you let destructive forces destroy, and
destroy, and destroy that which is constructive
in your world; but through your Call to your
"Beloved I AM Presence" and the "I AM
Presence" and Higher Mental Body of the Life
Streams whom you are trying to assist, you
demand the Great Central Sun's Cosmic Law of
Sacred Fire Love, Forgiveness, and Mercy which
seizes the attention of those who at the present
time will not do right. Ask the Sacred Fire to *seize
the attention!* Hold it upon the Sacred Fire until
enough of the consuming takes place to make
the individual awaken and release the feeling
within the emotional body to try to hold to the
constructive way of life.

Otherwise, My Dear Ones, there's no self-ef-
fort of the individual to overcome the evil that
has entrapped the outer self and holds it enslaved
to destruction. Unless some part of Life will pour
this Great Central Sun's Power Flame of the Sacred Fire's Love, Forgiveness, and Mercy to Life,
which the Violet Consuming Flame is, unless

that is concentrated somewhere in and around
individuals who are caught in the clutches of destructive forces, unless that comes forth, the
individual cannot free himself or herself by just
unascended demand. The Sacred Fire must come
and consume the connection between the outer
self and the mass accumulation of discord. Therefore It is the Redeeming Power of Life! It is the
All-purifying Sacred Fire! It is the All-wise, Bal-
ancing, Forgiving Force that is the Wisdom of
Life to use the Great Powers of the Sacred Fire
to cut Life free everywhere from human creation
that has been generated through the centuries. So
this is the way you cut yourselves free from all
connection with the mass accumulation of the
ages.

When you understand what's in the atmosphere of Earth, you will know how much
individuals in this world must have this if the
mass accumulation of hatred is to prevent the
destructive forces accomplishing their vicious
ends. Only the Sacred Fire from the Great Central Sun contains the Power of Love, Forgiveness,
and Mercy that consumes the human creation
and disconnects the outer self from the mass
pressure of the centuries! So tonight as you join

with Us and release now the Sacred Fire Love that demands the Freedom of all Life from all mankind's discord of the centuries, then when you say, "Save all—and 'all' contains my loved ones!" then the Cosmic Law would have to answer you, will have to save your loved ones, will have to give Assistance. Whether those Life Streams are embodied or disembodied matters not. The Love, Forgiveness, and Mercy of the Sacred Fire would have to flow in and around those Life Streams with whom you have been connected, and whose future you want to be the Victory of the Ascension.

So when you call for the Ascension of all Life everywhere in this world, and you demand whatever Great Central Sun's Sacred Fire Love, Forgiveness, and Mercy to Life, whatever Power of that Sacred Fire consumes human feeling, you have rendered a Service far beyond what you can understand tonight. And if you will say to the Great Cosmic Law: "Save my loved ones, and I will render Service to Life until all Life is purified, Ascended and Free!" And then the Cosmic Law can give you Miracles and Victories that you do not even dream could be accomplished in this life, even through those who at the present time seem caught in the clutches of destructive forces from which they cannot be free at the present moment.

This is sometimes referred to in religious channels as the vicarious atonement. It is not that. It is just obedience to the Great Law of Cause and Effect—that if you are interested in the Purification of all Life that all beings may have the Ascension—then your loved one is included in all, and must of necessity receive the sixty percent that is in your world. And your one wave of Love can be the Scepter of Power that determines the destiny of those who seem caught in the shadows, but who can be rescued by the Sacred Fire Love of Forgiveness and Mercy and Violet Flame Purification.

So Blessed Ones, go forward and be the Great Central Sun Magnet's Feeling of Love to Life that demands it be cut free from everything that is destructive, and that every Life Stream be forced to awaken and of its own Free Will, turn to the constructive way of life and give the obedience by which all human creation can be consumed forever. Then as you live in the World of the Sun Presence of Our Sacred Fire Love, Forgiveness, and Mercy to Life, you will understand why the

Violet Consuming Flame is the Royal Authority
and Power of the rulers of the world. Your
Mighty Saint Germain has poured this Love
throughout the ages. Now His Family of Violet
Flame Freedom I shall ever guard and offer
every possible Assistance until you all are willing
to do this. And in that will come the Fulfillment
of His Heart's Desire for the Purification and
Freedom of the Nation of His Heart—the Heart
of the World—and all Life is compelled to turn
away from the hordes of evil until they are
consumed, and Life Streams awakening, go
forward in the Obedience that does manifest
Perfection here that is the Ascension for all, not
only individuals, but the Powers of Nature, your
Nation, the world, and all upon it. And it is well
worth every effort of your Life to make this Call!
And your loved ones will be the beneficiaries as
well as the world.

So the Angels of Love and Mercy and For-
giveness are the Angels of the Violet Consuming
Flame. They are the Angels from the Healing
Temples of the Sacred Fire. They are the Sacred
Fire Angels of Eternal Purity. And all are so will-
ing and so ready to send forth on your slightest
Call this Power Flame of the Sacred Fire's Love,

Forgiveness, and Mercy to Life, and demand Purity in this world until there are no more shadows to cast discredit upon the Glory of the "Mighty I AM Presence" or cause distress to Life. So let Us all live that all suffering in all Life may now be consumed in the Sacred Fire's Violet Flame Love, Forgiveness, and Mercy to Life, and the Purity of Eternity come in now and be the only Healing Presence to the people of America and the world. And your loved ones shall one day stand with you in the Love and Gratitude of that Freedom, and Love will have claimed Its own into the Freedom of Eternity.

May you go forward and never forget this night, and never forget to call for all the Sacred Fire necessary to consume all mankind's human creation everywhere as soon as possible. I commend you to the Greatest Happiness you will ever know as you set this into action and see It force destructive forces into annihilation, and Life Streams thank you for Eternity for the Love of your Life which has opened the Door to their Freedom.

Thank you with all My Heart.

May Da Camara 1943

CHAPTER XIII

BELOVED MIGHTY VICTORY

Santa Fe, New Mexico
December 2, 1962
Record 934B; Cassette 60014

Beloved Ones of My Heart, in coming into the atmosphere of Earth to bring you Our Life Flame of Victory, I hope you'll understand that whatever We draw into this world must of necessity be the Sacred Fire Love of Our Life from the Ascended Masters' Octave. Therefore We cannot bring into outer physical conditions anything but the Sacred Fire Purity of Our Love that produces Victory. So when outer world conditions become discordant and chaotic, then as you call forth the All-purifying Christ into all physical conditions of this world, follow always with the acceptance and Release of all the Sacred Fire Love from Venus that compels Victory into everything that is constructive in manifestation in this world, compels

Victory and the Protection of that Victory around all who are trying to hold to the Light at this time, who are trying to be constructive, and who desire to be constructive. Now as you do this, you make yourselves the open door to which We can pour through you, to those conditions that are constructive, the Sacred Fire Love from Our Octave that will strengthen and protect everything that is constructive in every Life Stream—or things that are being created in this world.

Try to realize that whenever you call forth Our Victory into this world, It is the Release of the Sacred Fire of Our Life, Our Love, Our Purity. So as you call this into outer world conditions, automatically We must pour the same thing in and around you because you have called! You make yourselves an open door for Us to fill you with Our Life, the Victory of Our Life, the Victory of Our Sacred Fire Love. The more you call these conditions—the Cosmic Concentration of the various Activities of the Cosmic Christ— into outer world conditions, the more there must come in and around you the Ever-expanding World of Our Life, of Our Victory, of Our Love's Sacred Fire. So you cannot give this Protection to that which is constructive in the outer world without automatically having that Protection come in and around yourselves. So the most wonderful way to expand the Power of your own Protection is to keep calling forth into outer world conditions to protect everything that is constructive, and to prevent anything that's not constructive existing.

It doesn't make any difference whether you see the reason for it or not. In outer world conditions, no one from the appearance standpoint can judge what conditions are constructive and what are not. The appearance world does not tell you the Truth, does not show you the energy that is gathered at the Inner Level, and does not reveal the Light that is that which is constructive in every condition. Whenever there is anything constructive in any situation, that constructive energy is luminous from Our standpoint at the Inner Level; and people of the outer world cannot see that. That's why they do not judge correctly. When in handling situations of the outer world, they see only the appearance, and the appearance is changing so constantly that they cannot adequately approximate what is in a condition unless they were to see it from the Inner standpoint as We do.

But since it is not necessary for you to see everything from the Inner standpoint as We do, at least not at this time, as you call forth whatever Cosmic Christ Blue Lightning Purity is necessary into any condition in the physical world to force the Purification that compels the Victory of whatever is right to take place now in all outer physical conditions, so long as you demand the Immortal Victory of all that is right into outer world conditions. Then We can charge in and around you whatever We know is right for you to make you the Strength and the Power and the Victory of the Light that enables you to go forward and accomplish Miracles and Victories without limit—because you have drawn this into outer world conditions, and It must of necessity give you some of Itself. The Cosmic Law of giving is very wonderful! It's the Expanding Power of Life everywhere. Otherwise you would have no Expansion of Perfection.

So when conditions are not right in the outer, don't hesitate to just call whatever—if need be—World-enfolding Oceans of the Cosmic Christ Blue Lightning Purity necessary to prevent all evil, and replace it by whatever the Ascended Masters and Cosmic Beings know this world requires at this time to hold the Victory and the Protection of all that is constructive, and to be the Invincible Prevention of all that is of evil. We cannot and do not draw into this world anything except Our Sacred Fire All-purifying Love that wherever It goes, automatically prevents all wrong.

If people understood how to wrap themselves in Our World, Our Heart World of Sacred Fire Love from Venus, and blaze without reservation the Power of Our Invincible Heaven on Earth, Our Divine Plan Fulfilled Our Way that, just as It breathes into outer conditions, automatically dissolves and consumes and repels anything that is not the Purity of Our Sacred Fire Love! You will never know till your Ascension how important it is to call forth the "Beloved I AM Presence" and the Ascended Host, the Cosmic Beings' Cosmic Concentration of all the Sacred Fire Love necessary to purify the Earth, to prevent the existence of all wrong, and to bring into Manifestation in this world the Ascended Masters' Divine Plan fulfilled Their Way, the Ascended Masters' Heaven on Earth that is for Eternity Invincible against all wrong.

When you call Our Heaven on Earth into physical manifestations in this world, it doesn't make any difference what changes take place in the future, nothing can contaminate Our Heaven if We lower It into this octave. So It's the only Eternal Safety that you have! It's the only Eternal Protection that you have! It's the only Eternal Mastery that you have. It is not idly, I assure you, that We've been turning your attention to the use of the Ascended Masters' Heaven made physically manifest on Earth. We must begin to build this Perfection into this world, and then expand It as We keep calling forth the consuming of all the mistakes of the past.

Every time you consume destructive etheric records or anything that is mankind's miscreation, if you do not immediately replace it by Our Immortal Heaven on Earth, Invincible against all wrong forever; if you do not place It there, then more human creation can come in and occupy the place where the human creation had caused such discord. So when you speak of *the Ascended Masters' Divine Plan Fulfilled Their Way, that always manifests Their Invincible Heaven on Earth,* you can just as well call this into outer physical conditions to purify everything—bring all into Divine Order. You can balance everything; you can hold Protection for what is constructive, and if you don't bring this here, then human creation will flow in again, and again create discord.

So Blessed Ones, We are the only permanent correction of the conditions in this world that mankind has built which are so vicious and so frightfully destructive. And no matter how destructive they are or how vicious, when you call forth the Great Central Sun's Cosmic Christ Blue Lightning Purity that annihilates their viciousness out of the Universe for Eternity, It can strike! And when It strikes, It eats up the viciousness—compels its annihilation. But then as soon as that Purification takes place, replace it by the Ascended Masters' Divine Plan fulfilled Their Way, the Ascended Masters' Heaven on Earth Immortally Victorious over all human creation, and Immortally Free from anything that mankind would do in the future that would create discord. You must keep on commanding until everything is purified, and the world rebuilt into the original Perfection that was here before mankind manifested or embodied here.

The Great Beings who have created this world built a beautiful world, manifested for two million years everything of Beauty and Perfection and

Harmony—not one bit of discord. Mankind's needs were precipitated from the atmosphere, and that was the Original Divine Way to live Life, till mankind's attention wandered to the creation and was held there instead of remembering the Divine Pattern and the Divine Beings who had given all. From now on We must reverse what mankind has done, because We are in the Cycle of the Violet Consuming Flame wherein you are all authority—and so is the Violet Consuming Flame—to put an end to mankind's evil. And so when you call forth the Great Central Sun's Cosmic Concentration of the Violet Consuming Flame's All-purifying Sacred Fire Love that compels the prevention of all evil; and you demand the Ascended Masters' Heaven on Earth to manifest here as It did in the two first Golden Ages, wherever you abide, your experiences will be those of Our World. You will live, move, and have your beings in Our World of Permanent Harmony, Victorious Accomplishment, and Invincible Freedom from the distress that has tortured you through the centuries.

But you must command! You must take your stand! You must decide, and you must day after

day demand your being and world blasted free
forever from all connection with human discord
or human creation of any kind. We cannot do
that for you. We can pour Our Love and pour the
Violet Flame, but you are the authority by your
own Free Will to command what must be manifested where you abide.

So sometime every day, rise up into the Divine Dignity that is yours, the Divine Authority
of your "Beloved I AM Presence," and you decide, and you take your stand that you, your
"Beloved I AM Presence" and the Ascended
Host decide—demand, and command—that everything in your being and world must now
never be touched by human discord again! And
the more dynamic you get on that, the quicker
We can manifest It into your outer physical affairs. So it all depends upon you how soon you
want to be Free. *(applause)* Thank you so much.

Now when anything disturbs you in the outer
world, just turn away from it! Don't fight it! Turn
away from it! Go back to your "Presence" and
the Great Central Sun. Demand whatever Cosmic Concentration of the Violet Consuming
Flame's Victory of Sacred Fire Love compels
the prevention of all wrong from touching you

or your world or your loved ones, or anything you care to accomplish. It won't take but a very short time for you to form this habit, and it will bring you the greatest Joy and sense of Freedom you have ever known. And I hope you experiment with it over the next two or three weeks before Christmas so We can bring you an amazing Christmas Gift! *(applause)* Thank you so much, Precious Ones. Won't you be seated, please, and just remain so.

I hope We may have the privilege, not too far hence, of amazing you with some Miracles and Victories which the Angels of Victory from Venus produce in this world which are part of the Divine Plan's Fulfillment which They bring from Venus; and which will bring such Happiness as you will not know until you begin to see the Manifestations for which you call come into your beings and worlds, and give you the Blessings which They are. We have Boundless Blessings, Precious Ones. We have all the Miracles of Perfection for Eternity! Venus knows no discord. Isn't that wonderful to think there's someplace in the Universe—*(applause)* Thank you so much.

And I want so much to free you all from the struggle, the discord, the problems, the daily

strain which was never God created, never intended, was never the part of the Divine Plan. So
now I have your welfare at Heart! I want you to
be Our Family of Happiness, and I want to show
you the Miracles from Venus that must be built
into this world. And that's why I'm here drawing you on by giving you a little insight into that
which We want to bring into this physical world
permanently. The Angels of Victory from Venus
are the Bearers of that Perfection. They are My
Family that will bring you My Way of Life. They
are My Family of Love Supreme, and They are
so willing to associate with you. Isn't that wonderful? *(applause)* Thank you so much.

They are so willing to give you what They
have! This world needs It so much, but it must
be purified and cleansed first, and the way provided for these Blessings to come and be built
into this world as an eternal part of Life's Great
Love and Perfection to all who pass this way—and
that shall ever illumine everything that comes
into physical embodiment. So Blessed Ones,
when you begin to demand the Cosmic Illumination of the Angels of Victory from Venus, you
shall have Illumination! The world shall have
Illumination! And I assure you, in that Illumina-

tion will be very great Joy, because into It the shadows of human creation can never approach. So We offer you Our World of Security, Our Realm of Freedom, Our Miracles and Victory of the Love that has so long maintained Perfection on Venus. And now It must come into this world and make this world, too, a Sun of the Love of the Sacred Fire and Its Almighty Blessing to Life; so Life that comes here knows no distress, but moves forward into the Fulfillment of the Divine Plan of the Ascension.

I shall await with very Great Joy your Call for this to come into the physical octave where you abide, and then We can expand that to help the rest of mankind awaken as soon as possible; for all must awaken to the Love from Venus that wants to bring here the Divine Plan's Fulfillment—Our Realm of Life, Our Invincible Heaven on Earth—and close the door of memory, of feeling, of experience to all that is not the Love and the Victory of Our Perfection in the future.

So Blessed Ones, you have a marvelous vista ahead of you of all the Perfection Life has planned for you here; and if you care to call this into outer action, you will give Us the opportunity to bring at least in and around you as quickly as possible those Blessings that are to become Eternal to this Earth. I commend you to the Love in the Hearts of the Angels of Victory from Venus! And may your association with Them ever bring you the Mightiest Joy of all Eternity. Thank you with all My Heart.

CHAPTER XIV

BELOVED ARCHANGEL MICHAEL

Chicago, Illinois
April 21, 1963
Record CD1021; Cassette 60182

Beloved Ones of My Heart, I wish to bring to your attention this hour, and for your use, more of the Power from Our Ascended Master Octave that you do require in this world, that the world itself requires, and that can do for you that which only the Power of the Angelic Host can do. You have been giving recognition to the Master Flame. This moment I ask you to give recognition to the *Master Power of the entire Angelic Host* to come into this world, and blaze whatever Sacred Fire Power and Presence into this world compels the Purification which must come!

When We offer you the Power of the Angelic Host, that is from not only the Ascended Beings; but the Power of the Sacred Fire of the Angelic

Host means all the Power that has been used through aeons of time by those Great Beings who are Angels, but who have never yet embodied in human form. There are Uncountable Legions of the Angels of the Sacred Fire created by the Cosmic Beings to render that Service in the use of the Sacred Fire which is concerned with the creation of a planet or a system of worlds. There are Uncountable Legions of the Sacred Fire of the Angelic Host; and when I ask you to call forth the Master Power of all the Angelic Host, it includes all who are Ascended—and the Cosmic Beings' Power that the Angelic Host wield who as yet have never been in physical embodiment. Therefore They are the Master Presence of such Purity, such Love, and such Power of the Sacred Fire that the human intellect cannot comprehend It, until you see It in action or you feel It enfold you and make you realize the Presence which It is.

This world and mankind upon it have been the focus of tremendous energy drawn here for manifestation, some through the Powers of Nature, some through the Beings who direct the Powers of Nature, some through mankind, some through the atmosphere of Earth. Some energy

that's poured forth into this world is the Great
Cosmic Light Rays, the Cosmic Rays that have
been made permanent to the Earth in Their
Blessing to purify and stabilize the flow of Life
in this world. There are the natural Rays that
have been made permanent to this world. There
are the Cosmic Rays that have poured and are
pouring certain Currents of the Sacred Fire—and
the Great Cosmic Electronic Force from the
Physical Sun and the Great Central Sun—into
outer world physical conditions for the manifestation of Perfection, and not for mankind's
misuse of the energy of Life!

Since the pressure of the energy mankind has
misused and qualified with destruction is reaching the bursting point at certain points on the
surface of the Earth, We wish to draw in,
through, and around you as much as possible the
greater Release of the Power of the Angelic Host
to hold control of certain manifestations that you
can contact, and that you need to draw into
outer physical conditions to help you master the
destructive forces that are here generated by
mankind.

When you begin to call forth the Master Powers of Life, the Master Flame, the Master

Qualities, the Master Powers of Consciousness, you need always to recognize that those special Activities of Life from the Ascended Masters' Octave are always the Flow of certain Powers of the Sacred Fire. All the Sacred Fire is consciously directed by Intelligent Beings, whether They be Ascended or those originally created to use that Power in a system of worlds to bring forth the Manifestation of Perfection here. As you give this recognition, you can have drawn in and around you by Our Concentration—through your Calls— of certain Activities of the Sacred Fire from Our Octave that are an Enfolding Power of Protection, because the Sacred Fire is the only Master Presence of mankind's human creation here. The Sacred Fire is the Activity of the Cosmic Life from the Great Central Sun that is provided to create, hold sustained, keep in action and controlled the manifestations of systems of worlds. Therefore you, being an individual system of worlds within yourselves, must come under that same Law as the planetary systems.

I want you to begin to feel, by your own Conscious Call, the greater Power that We want to pour in and around you to help you do what service you're rendering in the physical world with greater ease and comfort, with less strain, and with Protection and Victory always. You must have Power in and around yourselves, Beloved Ones, to both survive and to accomplish that which you're trying to do in the physical world to fulfill the Divine Plan. You must have the Power of the Sacred Fire if you're going to master manifestation in this world that is discordant.

So when you begin to call forth the Angelic Host's Master Power of the Violet Consuming Flame, you will find It is the concentration and condensation of certain Activities of the Violet Consuming Flame which We hold in the atmosphere of Earth and which govern the system itself. You can just as well have an individualized Stream of that to flow in and around you to sustain certain activities wherein you need more Power. And the Power you need is the Violet Consuming Flame's Control of manifestation. That Blessed Violet Consuming Flame has so many Blessings within It! It has so many Activities that produce only Perfection, that We want you, by your own use of the Master Power of the Violet Consuming Flame's Control of manifestation, to experiment with this, use It to accomplish what you wish to do in the physical world, fill yourselves with It so you feel the Power of Its Mastery. And you must feel It before It can act in the outer to control conditions that surround you.

There are many reasons why I'm asking for this this moment, because if you call It in and around yourselves as the All-controlling Sun Presence of the Violet Consuming Flame's Force that rules manifestation, It can be for you a world of your own, your own individual Protection. So the Master Power of the Violet Consuming Flame's Protecting Presence can be drawn in and around you by your own Conscious Call, by your demand for Its Concentration, and by the Angels, the Cosmic Angels of the Violet Consuming Flame's Power of Love that, enfolding you in Itself, disconnects you from the pressure and the substance that mankind has qualified with hatred, discord, and impurity.

So I would deeply appreciate your calling forth the Master Power of the Violet Consuming Flame which the Cosmic Angels of Its Presence concentrate into physical conditions to hold greater Control over disturbing elements. This is just as if you wielded a searchlight, and you sent it anywhere that you wanted to observe things that you wanted to use. As you call forth the Cosmic Angels of the Violet Flame Master Power into any physical condition to produce the Violet Consuming Flame's Perfection there, demand that It be established as an Eternal Manifestation in and around yourselves or in conditions with which you are concerned.

Whatever you call forth, call forth the Eternal Manifestations of the Violet Consuming Flame's Master Power to control the physical manifested Universe. This, if you already had a Momentum of this around you, would control the storm, would control the waves, would control the wind, and would control many physical conditions around you in which you move every day and do not realize how much they impose their discord upon you. This has many almost Infinite Blessings that are the most practical thing you can ever use of Life's Powers—the most practical Powers of Life that you can use to control physical conditions in which you move and must live.

You have the sinister force mass accumulation of discord trying to rule this, that, and the other thing, and trying to bring forth more and more destruction—directed by human beings! We want to train you to direct the Master Power and the Master Powers of the Angels of the Violet Consuming Flame's Almighty Miracle Manifestations into the world around you to fill your world with that which the outer world cannot give you. *(applause)* Thank you so much. Won't you be seated, please.

Now if you care to demand that everything in your being and world be filled with *now* the Miracle Manifestations of the Violet Consuming Flame's Master Power that hold in and around you the Gifts and the Activities and the Blessings of the Violet Flame Angels—some of those are Ascended Beings, some are not—but if you will demand that your world be peopled with those Beings of the Violet Consuming Flame who are the Master Control of manifestation in this world, wherever They go, They will control the manifestation in which you move. They are Masters of it by the Sacred Fire. Now I'm not intruding into the Mighty Saint Germain's Domain by any means, but We all are in the Realm of the Violet Consuming Flame, and We all direct It because of Its Miracle Cosmic Action to control manifestation.

If you will demand that your world manifest as a Violet Flaming Sun Presence of the Master

Control, the Ascended Masters' Sacred Fire Control of manifestation, My Dear Ones, you have no idea, if you will call this into action—call the Angels of the Violet Flame to be the Master Control around your automobiles, around everybody and everything you contact, around everything in which you must move—you will find the sinister force cannot connect with you or produce the conditions that either become your problems or sometimes your destruction. And there is nothing you need more right now than the continual, Ever-expanding Protection of the Sacred Fire—of which the Violet Consuming Flame is one Activity.

If I were you, moving as you have to in the outer world among discordant conditions that are produced by other individuals, you do not necessarily need to contact those conditions if your own world is insulated in the Master Presence of the Violet Consuming Flame's Invincible Control of manifestation by the Violet Flame Angels' Sacred Fire Love. If I were you, I would charge every automobile that you have, every means of conveyance—if you're on an airplane, if you're in a train, if you're moving in automobiles or buses anywhere, anything that you're doing in motion

in the physical world—get in the habit of de-
manding the Violet Flame Angels' Master Power
and Master Presence of Eternal Control of that
manifestation. Then that can never affect you
discordantly. But if you do not sustain It, call for
It as Eternal Control, you might control it one
day, and if your attention is off of it and you're
not keeping the attention on the "Presence" or
the Violet Flame, the next day, if you're unaware
of this Enfolding Violet Flame Master Power or
you become irritated, you can again connect
with destructive forces. But if you make this a
habit of feeling and seeing, moving within and
using the Master Power of the Violet Consuming Flame's Control of all manifestation, your
very awareness of that and your Love to the
Angels of the Violet Flame can be for you an Invincible Protection until you stand Ascended and
Free. That can be your world of experience. It
can be your world's control of other manifestations in this world. It can be your world's control
of things that affect you.

I'm trying to get this into your consciousness
today so that you feel you live within a Sun Presence of the Master Power of the Violet Flame
Love—which the Hearts of the Violet Flame

Angels concentrate in and around you—and that
controls conditions many times of which you're
totally unaware. If you were to call this forth
also, and I feel sure you all will, to fill yourselves
with the Master Power of the Violet Consuming
Flame's Love from the Healing Angels who use
It for healing, fill yourselves with It, and command It to do Its Perfect Work by not only your
own "Mighty I AM Presence" but Their Love.
They exist just to give Their Love through using
the Violet Consuming Flame. It is Their Love
that controls the manifestations of the physical
world. It is Their Love that enfolds the plant life
and repels discordant conditions that otherwise
would destroy it. Their Love can just as well
enfold you.

Now this is not to teach you to lean on any-
body or anything but your "Presence." But your
"Beloved I AM Presence"—after you've called to
It and the Mighty Saint Germain—They have
Ways and Means of fulfilling your Calls. And the
Violet Flame Angels are those Blessed Beings who
produce the Manifestation that does fulfill your
Call, that fulfills the Command of the Mighty
Saint Germain or the Command of your "Pres-
ence" or the Command of any Ascended Being.

So learn to call forth the Master Power of the Cosmic Violet Flame Angels' Love in and around you, and see for yourselves whether They're real or not. See whether They can make you feel Their Presence. See whether They can control conditions. And if you ask to see that, if you ask to see the Fulfillment of your Calls, one day, and sometimes when you least expect it, the atmosphere of Earth will part and you will see Them face to face doing the very thing that fulfills your Call. I want you to have that! *(applause)* Thank you.

Now just one more thing. Do you know, under the Action of the Cosmic Law, that when an unascended being calls to an Angel of the Violet Consuming Flame to purify a condition or control it so destructive forces cannot act, do you know, the Cosmic Law is such that They have to fulfill your Call. They cannot refuse. Therefore, you have an absolute certainty of Their Assistance to you, and one day you can have the joyous experience of seeing Them stand beside you and control manifestations that otherwise might destroy you. So Beloved Ones, I want you to become acquainted with the Cosmic Violet Flame Angels' Master Power of the Love that rules, molds, sustains, and eternally controls the manifested Universe. These are a Mighty Powerhouse for the Violet Consuming Flame's Limitless Gifts and Love to Life—and Limitless Power of Victory. You can't possibly fail if you become aware of Their Presence!

And just for your own satisfaction, if you will take something that you use every day and ask your "Beloved I AM Presence" and the Mighty Saint Germain, or even Myself, to charge that with the Eternal Memory to call the Violet Flame Angels' Love and the Power, the Master Power of the Violet Consuming Flame in and around you sometime each day; if you care to take something and use it as a reminder to give this Acknowledgement—something that you have to use every day—then you get so that when you see that you will remember to give Acknowledgement to that Flame until it comes to the time when you can see It around yourselves. This is just a thought to help you remember, because the outer world's constant pull upon you continually makes you forget. And if you do happen to have a habit of forgetting, *(laughter)* let Us do this: Charge your feeling and your mind, the brain structure, with the

Master Power of the Sacred Fire's Immortal Purity that always lets your Higher Mental Body make you remember that which will help you and bless you. You know, it's just as important to charge yourselves with the Ascended Masters' Consciousness of Eternal Divine Memory and the Consciousness that makes you forget what you should forget—and remember what you should remember!

So this use of the Violet Consuming Flame's Master Power of the Control of manifestation will, I'm sure, bring you very great Joy. Just acknowledge It. Ask your "Beloved I AM Presence" and the Mighty Saint Germain to fill you with It as They use It. Then call the Cosmic Angels of the Violet Consuming Flame's Master Power to blaze in and around you, and keep on blazing Their Hearts' Love of the Control of all manifestation— Their Hearts' Master Power of Violet Consuming Flame's Immortal Protection around you and around everything you use, around everybody you contact, until you become so blazing with the Concentration of that Power that that which is of discord cannot come near you. Therefore you are increasing your Protection as you render service in the outer world that sometimes will hold your

attention and use your energy when you're busy
doing something; and yet the Violet Consuming
Flame's Master Power that you have gathered as
a Momentum stands ever your Guard, and the
Angelic Host abide with you until your service is
rendered.

You only need to try it a few times. When you
start out in your day's activities or you go to sleep
at night or sometimes in the midst of something
else, just ask a Sun Presence of the Master Power
of the Violet Flame Love from the Cosmic Angels to flow in and around you and be established
there permanently. Just try it! You don't need to
ask for any particular thing. Just ask that it be
established as a Sun Presence around you and
become eternally at One with your Life Stream,
forever expands, but is the Controlling Master
Power by the Violet Consuming Flame's Love
that rules manifestation. This is what you want if
you are going to prevent the destructive activities of physical conditions in the physical world.

And if you should care to call forth the Cosmic
Legions of the Violet Consuming Flame's Great
Angelic Host of such Master Power, such Concentration of that Violet Consuming Flame as
shall make the Earth tremble, you can have that

drawn around you to make everything obey the Love that is its Master. And that can be done! It has been done, and sometimes it's necessary to do it in order to shake mankind awake to the place where it forces destructive forces to be seized and bound to prevent the evil they intend. If I were you, I would ask this Nation be filled with the Master Power of the Violet Consuming Flame's terrific Sacred Fire Control of all manifestation within your Land, and then call the Limitless Cosmic Legions of the Angels of the Violet Flame to come in and be the Rulers and the Controllers of all action in the physical world within your Nation. And you will never have cause to regret It. Never!

I'm giving you something that you can use, you need, and that is absolutely infallible in Its Control of conditions of the outer world as they exist today. *(applause)* Thank you so much,   Precious Ones. So now when you think of that Beloved Violet Consuming Flame, send your Love always to the Cosmic Legions of the Cosmic Angels who are the Cosmic Guard of this planet and the manifestations upon it; and ask that Their Master Power of Their Love enfold you in whatever intensity of that Violet

Consuming Flame They know will control conditions in which you move and prevent anything
else touching you.

So I come to help you establish this; and I
shall be ready to assist in any way I can if you
will remember to do It—if you call It into action,
if you command It to be sustained, and if you
remember to send those Cosmic Beings, those
Blessed Angels, your Love to enable Them to
fulfill the Great Divine Plan. I enfold you in the
Master Power of the Violet Consuming Flame's
Love which the Cosmic Angels direct to control
manifestation everywhere about you, to enfold
you in Their Victory, and to keep you from feeling the disturbance and the distress in the outer
world. May you dwell within the Peace of Their
Hearts, in the Love of Their Power, and in the
Victory of Their Sacred Fire Presence; and call
Them into the lower physical atmosphere of
Earth to render that Service which They alone
can give, which the world needs, and which
brings the Victorious Control of outer world
conditions everywhere at your Command.

And We shall *never* be found wanting! So I
offer you more Protection, that you may help to
control the physical conditions in this world to

prevent the discord that otherwise will manifest. So with My own Heart's Flame of the Love for that Violet Consuming Flame, I offer you Its Master Presence to enfold you, to protect you, to illumine you, to make you Victorious, to ever abide with you as an eternal part of your own Life's Flame, and the outer self be held within Its Glorifying, Victorious Power forever. Thank you with all My Heart.

BELOVED COSMIC ANGEL

CHAPTER XV

GREAT COSMIC ANGEL
ON WHOSE CROWN BLAZES THE WORD
"UNION"

Chicago, Illinois
June 25, 1964
Record CD 1048

Blessed, Beloved Ones of Our Hearts, I wish to assure you tonight that Our Love for you is beyond anything you can understand in your willingness to stand and give these Decrees for the Purification, Protection, and Freedom of the Nation that is the Heart of the World. I wish to reveal something to you tonight that perhaps will give you some concept of what terrific effort Life goes to in order to not only sustain a planet and Life upon It, but to help the beings who embody here to fulfill the Great Divine Plan that raises them unto the Ascension.

Could you see as We do the accumulation of mankind's discord which always creates darkness—it's just like soot in the atmosphere of a city. Mankind's discord is an impurity, and therefore when at intervals the Great Cosmic Law permits the Cosmic Beings to consume a certain proportion, or perhaps all of the discord accumulated up to that time, it is because the planet and mankind upon it could not survive if a certain proportion of that impurity is not taken off at intervals.

Now this is what affects the planet, but the same thing is true of the individual. If a certain accumulation of discord in the emotional body, the feeling world of the individual, is not removed from time to time, it accumulates to the point where it makes it impossible for the Light within the Unfed Flame in the Heart to expand enough through the outer self to hold Its Activities to the constructive way of life. We govern the Destiny of individual Life Streams as well as the Destiny of a nation. Each nation has a Cosmic Being and Legions of the Angelic Host who are the Governing Intelligence to try to purify each nation and help it to arise to the Fulfillment of its Divine Plan. Just as your Higher Mental Body is the Guarding Presence for the outer self and its activities as you go through many embodiments, so is there provided for each nation a

Guarding Presence of that nation to hold its identity, until it either fulfills the Divine Plan, or its discord dissolves it, and it loses its identity as the centuries go on.

The Angelic Host's Service to Life is beyond anything you can comprehend! And may I give you just a little of the Joy that is Ours when We see a group of people harmonized long enough to let the Light expand through each one, and as the group hold together, each one's Life Stream pours a Flame into the combined energy; and that becomes a Sun Presence of Power of constructive action that that group can bring into outer physical conditions. This is how constructive activity through the centuries is brought into outer world experience in one civilization after another. All the constructive ideas in every civilization are given to the humanity within that civilization by not only the Higher Mental Body of each Life Stream, but the Ascended Host and the Cosmic Beings who are trying to expand the Light through every Heart Flame—the Light through every nation, the Light through the substance and structure of Earth itself; until it becomes luminous to the point where the Life Streams embodying here can never again create discord.

This is the way We give Protection to everything that is constructive. Therefore when you think of Protection, will you always think of a Sun Presence of one or more Activities of the Sacred Fire that goes forth in answer to your Call. And if you could see this once from the Inner Level, you'd be the happiest people on Earth! When your Heart's Flame reaches up to your "Presence," your "Mighty I AM Presence" or the Ascended Host, and you call the various activities of the Sacred Love of the Sacred Fire into the conditions of the physical world to enfold individuals or localities or activities of the outer life, the moment your Heart desires to render that Service, the Heart's Flame Itself sends up Its own Ray of Light and Love, and your "Beloved I AM Presence" and the Ascended Host take that up, and pouring Their own Sacred Fire's Love into It, amplify It into a Sun Presence, and project It forth on a Light Ray into a condition or in and around individuals or localities to bring Perfection from the Ascended Masters' Octave into this world.

This goes on all the time, and is the Great Law of Life's Ever-expanding Perfection to bless unascended beings with enough of the Sacred

Fire Love from the Ascended Masters' Octave to be the Magnetic Pull that draws the individual Heart Flame up and out of the clutches of human creation. Therefore when you wish to free individuals from destructive conditions, try to remember, your "Mighty I AM Presence" and one or more of the Ascended Host must at all times pour forth some Activity of the Sacred Fire or Cosmic Light from the Ascended Masters' Octave into this world to master conditions here–to establish here the Perfection from Our Octave that is the Fulfillment of the Divine Plan to lift the individual or the condition out of the control of destructive forces.

When this is the condition that affects an entire Nation, I'm sure you can begin to realize now something of how gigantic is the task to purify this Nation. And this Nation has the most Light of any nation in the world! You can begin to see what it means, from Our Standpoint, to draw enough of the Cosmic Sacred Fire Purity of Our Love, and concentrate It into a nation and into the people of a nation to stand aside enough of the destructive forces to let that which is the constructive activity within each Life Stream render its service to the Nation, and through the Nation to the world.

The Ever-expanding Perfection of Life is carried on continually by the Expansion of the Light from within the Heart. The Expansion of the Light from within the Sevenfold Flame in the forehead of the individual goes forth into the mental and feeling world of a mass of the people, carrying the Consciousness of the Seven Mighty Elohim and Their Constructive Ideas and Ways and Means of creating—producing Perfection in the physical octave without strain nor struggle. The only thing that makes strain, struggle or limitation is the discord in the feeling. If there be discord in the picture in the mind, it always remains in the mental realm until the energy in the feeling world concentrates upon that picture and condenses until it becomes substance. Then that becomes a thing manifest.

The Angelic Host are continually pouring the Energy of Their Love, the Energy of Their Life, in and around anybody and anything that will remain harmonious enough to let It come in, flow through the individual, produce Perfection, and expand through the individual to flow on Its Way to produce more Perfection in the world around you. Now I wish you to understand how limitless is Life, and how magnificent is the

Great Plan of Ever-expanding Perfection to all Life everywhere. Suppose you need some Assistance from your "Beloved I AM Presence" and the Ascended Host. You make your Call. The Heart Flame of your Higher Mental Body floods through this outer self, producing Harmony, Purity, and the Patterns of Perfection into your outer self; and then that acts through you to create certain things in the physical world. But that Heart Flame continues to flow on until It fills the world with that same Perfection also. And then It continues to flow until It produces similar Perfection in the system.

There is no stopping and no end to the Expansion of the Perfection that comes from within the Heart Flame of the Sacred Fire's Life of the individual, and that's something to study! That's a concept mankind needs to understand! That is the Infinite Power of the Life of the Universe; and that is what sustains a world or a system of worlds in Its Great Cosmic Action and Fulfillment of the Divine Plan, till everything becomes Self-luminous and pours Its Light of the Love of Life into the Infinite Space around the planet or the system. And It goes on and on and on, ever expanding Its Blessing and Perfection to Life wherever It goes in Infinite Space. Thus you have the Infinite, Eternal, Ever-expanding Presence of Perfection without limit, Mastery without limit, Happiness without limit, and the Ever-raising, Illumining Power that raises all into the Ascension, wherein Creation goes on in ever greater and greater Magnificent Manifestation—with never a discord to be experienced again.

It is worth every effort you could ever make to understand this Law and realize how Eternal is the Ever-expanding Sacred Fire Love's Perfection of Life! If We did not understand the Eternal Law concerning Manifestation, it would be very difficult to watch mankind go on century after century in the denial of the Perfection that everywhere in Infinite Space reveals this Law. There is no excuse for any human being on this Earth being either an atheist or battling the Great Perfection of Life. Whole systems of worlds—galaxies of systems of worlds—are ever holding Divine Order and Balance in Infinite Space and ever giving their Light to the Universe around them. There is no excuse for mankind's lack of understanding of the magnitude of Life, Its Limitless Blessings, and Its Activity of Ever-creating, Expanding Perfection that cannot produce discord anywhere in creation. Unascended beings can understand this if they want to!

So to you I come tonight and offer the Love of My own Heart's Flame to be the Fulfillment of the Fiat I issued for the Fulfillment of the Destiny of this Nation, and to release the Power by which that Destiny becomes manifest. When benighted individuals in other parts of the world think they're going to either destroy or desecrate this Nation that is the Heart of the World, they are badly mistaken! *(applause)* Thank you so much, Precious Ones. Won't you be seated, please, and just remain so.

I just happen to be one of the Guardians of this Nation, and if unascended beings think they're going to destroy or desecrate the Handiwork of Cosmic Beings who have created this Nation, created the world and placed the Blessings of Life upon It, then individuals must be shocked awake by their own creation. And human creation is perfectly capable of awakening the consciousness of an individual who is bound in the darkness of selfishness, and wishes to impose its discord upon other Life Streams. So it would pay everybody to be invincibly, eternally honest with the Fiery Truth of the Great Heart Flame of Life that produces only Perfection, sustains It for Eternity, expands It without limit, and is the Master Hand of Creation through individual Life Streams who are using the Life of the Universe.

Individuals' own Life Streams are not their life unless they serve the constructive way of life! They better get this tonight! Because individuals are bound in the selfishness and darkness of their own discord doesn't mean that the Great Cosmic Beings that rule the system of worlds—the Great Cosmic Legions of the Angels of the Sacred Love of the Sacred Fire, or the Great Cosmic Beings who have drawn the Electronic Force that makes the Physical Sun, have drawn that into existence, sustained It and let Its Life flow forth to the system; poor, benighted mankind is in darkness indeed when individuals think they can interfere with that Great Presence of Life's Perfection!

I want you to feel encouraged tonight because since I am one of the Guardians of this Nation and you are atoms in the body of this Nation, I am one of those who is a Guardian of each of you. You didn't know you had individual Guardians, but it's true! Otherwise your life might not receive all the Assistance that you need at this particular time to let the Light be the Strength in the American people to throw off what seeks to desecrate and destroy them.

When you wish Protection for the Nation, call the Sacred Fire of My Life into the physical octave and the physical conditions of this Nation with the Cosmic Fiat for the Great Central Sun's Eternal Purity to blaze the Flame that possesses and rules all, and manifests the Fulfillment of the Divine Plan wherever you call It into action. I can wield Unlimited Power! I can give you everything that is constructive! I am thoroughly aware of all that is within the Nation, and also, I know what's in the intent of the sinister force and the unfortunate individuals who are the pawns of its destruction. When individuals think they're going to wreck this Nation, they do not understand what is Greater than themselves. Of course, that's not to be wondered at; but nevertheless, those who have sworn to destroy you shall have their destruction bound back into them, and their own evil will destroy itself! *(applause)* Thank you so much.

Now one thing I want to remind you of a warning for Eternity. Whenever you are successful and the answers to your Calls have come, become more and more humble, more and more grateful, and more and more harmonious and obedient to the "Presence" and the Ascended Host! Don't ever be tempted to gloat over anything that is your success. There is no quicker way the sinister force can trap you than through the feeling of exploiting the Victory that the "Presence" and the Ascended Host have created and released in and around you in the Fulfillment of your Calls. If you remain humble in the hour of your greatest Victory, you will *always* have Protection. When anything of the outer self wants to lord it over somebody else, failure is right then in the individual.

Beloved Ones, I give this to you as a matter of Protection. If in the outer self—when the Mighty Saint Germain gave you this in the beginning—if in every thought, feeling, spoken word, and act of the outer self, credit were given to the "Beloved I AM Presence" as the Doer, Miracles unbelievable would take place. Therefore when you have called to the Ascended Host for the Release of the Powers that correct physical conditions and then you see that condition corrected, remember, the Victory belongs to the

"Presence" and the Ascended Host whose Life Flame and Love from Their Hearts went into the condition to correct it. So the Victory belongs always to the "Beloved I AM Presence" and the Sacred Fire Love of the Ascended Host.

We have given you many times the Call for Love, Forgiveness, and Mercy to dissolve and consume human creation; and I tell you frankly, someday, sometime, somewhere, everything on this Earth that is of human discord must be dissolved by the Sacred Fire's Purifying Love, the Love that consumes destructive forces, that their suffering may cease. So when your opportunity is so great to call forth the Heart Flames from the Ascended Masters of Their Miracle Love and Sacred Fire Manifestations into yourselves and into your affairs, into your Nation, and into all Life that you contact, if you will only let that expand, It will fill you with such Miracles and such Freedom in the use of the Great Master Powers of your own "Beloved I AM Presence" as shall lift you above every limitation in this world.

Blessed Ones, I could talk forever on the Blessings that will be yours when you begin to call forth into yourselves—first, through yourselves, around yourselves, and into your affairs—the Heart Flames of Sacred Fire Love from, of course, always your "Presence" first, but from the Ascended Masters and Cosmic Beings, to create Eternal Perfection in this world and into all Life that you contact. Your business in Life is to expand Perfection to the rest of Life, and that Perfection is Eternal and Ever-expanding. That's the Law of the Universe. It's the Law of all constructive action.

When you make up your mind that that is to be your daily habit, that's to be the routine of your use of Life every day, nothing could be denied you; and you would automatically have your world filled with the same Great Heart Flame of Sacred Fire Love that you call forth into outer physical conditions. If you care to experiment with this and establish this as a Heart Flame around your physical body, and realize that you abide within that, and wherever you go, you live in the Heart Realm of Life. Then you pour forth to the rest of Life your Heart's Command to Life. And when you choose to use the Heart Flame's Sacred Fire Love from any Ascended Master or Cosmic Being—from any of the Angelic Host—you have but to make the Call, and the Flame descends, and Love answers Its own instantly.

It is very much more enjoyable, I assure you, to go through this world and fill it with the Heart Flame of Sacred Fire Love from your "Presence" and the Ascended Host, than go through your daily experiences of struggle and strain and problems and mistakes and limitations and the conditions that you have experienced up until now. But those conditions can cease from this hour if you care to reach up and accept this which I offer, this which I have the Authority and Power to release into you and through you and into your affairs, in your conditions, and into the Nation, as the Power of the Ascended Masters' Life that saves the Nation from the discord mankind has imposed upon it.

Beloved Ones, as you continue to call to the Angelic Host for Their Sacred Fire Control of manifestations here, you will be the happiest people that ever drew breath in this world! And I just want you to remain happy for Eternity, so let us use It from tonight! *(applause)* Thank you so much. Now there's one more thing. From the outer self's standpoint of the feeling world, it's not easy when people are discordant and imposing downright discord upon you, to call Divine Love to bless them. We appreciate that, but if you

will still yourselves first; fill yourselves with Our
Hearts' Flame of Sacred Fire Love; and ask Us
to wrap the other individual or the condition in
Our Hearts' Flame of Sacred Fire Love—as you
call It into yourselves, first of all you disconnect
your own Life energy from the condition. And
if you ask Us to wrap the condition in Our Sacred Fire's Love, We can do It! That Sacred Fire
Love will change the condition when you in the
emotional body, because of your own feeling
world, cannot do it.

I do not mean that you shouldn't try; but if
you'll only realize that the Sacred Fire Love from
an Ascended Master's Heart is the Master Control of manifestation in this world, you will hold
yourselves filled with that. You will feel It around
you, and then you ask It to go forth and bless the
rest of Life, and you have complied with the
Great Law of Love. That's what makes you Master over the manifested Universe. That is what
enables you to wield Unlimited Power, and at the
same time be kept Eternally, Invincibly Protected.

There is no Power superior to the Heart Flame
of Eternal Love! Whether that Heart Flame
comes from your "Beloved I AM Presence" or

the Hearts of the Ascended Host or the Heart
Flame of the Physical Sun or the Heart Flame of
the Great Central Sun matters not—the Heart
Flames of the Angelic Host. There is the one
Master Presence and Power of Life to which everything in the manifested Universe bows and
gives Obedience, and It's the only thing worth
serving. From tonight, I trust you will experiment
with this! If you choose to live in Our Heart
Realm of Our Hearts' Sacred Fire Love to enfold
you in Our World of Its Eternal Perfection, wherever you abide Life will be purified, harmonized,
blessed, and raised into the harmonious way of
association with you.

It is the way you can harmonize your world
for Eternity, and not be subject to the limitations
or the distress of the present conditions in the
outer world. So We hope you will let Us insulate
you in the Sacred Fire Love of Our own Hearts'
Realm of Life, and let Our Ascended Master
Power and Presence of that Sacred Fire Love
pour Its Eternal Blessing and Perfection in and
around you, and become an eternal part of your
Life Stream as you give It to the rest of the
world; till this world becomes a Sun Presence of
Its Victory also.

So We commend you to the enjoyment of using the Master Power of Life's Almighty Victory and Control of the manifested Universe by the only thing that permits it to exist. May you go forward and live in the Heart Realm of Our Sacred Fire Love, the Sacred Fire Love of your "Presence," and let Us show you what Magnificent Blessings await your use, and what Magnificent Temples of the Sacred Fire become your Powerhouse of Manifestation to give to the rest of Life the Happiness of Eternity. Go forward and dwell with Us in Our World of the Heart's Love to Life, and you will never have cause to regret it. Thank you with all My Heart.

CHAPTER XVI

BELOVED MARY

Chicago, Illinois
December 24, 1964
Record CD 1114

Precious Beloved Hearts of the Love from the Heart of Creation! We come tonight to again intensify as much of that Sacred Fire in the lower atmosphere of Earth as possible at this time. We want you all to feel the nearness of Our Presence, because it is in your feeling world that We must render the Greatest Service possible to help you. It is in the emotional bodies of the people that the Love is needed because the intellect cannot love. All the intellect can do—except in the sense that it creates pictures of Perfection, and enjoys the picturing of Perfection; and that is, of course, an action of Love—but the intense Power of the Sacred Fire Love of the Universe is in the emotional body through the Heart.

The Love that pours forth from the permanent atom in the Heart as It fills the emotional body is the Ever-expanding Sacred Fire Power from the Heart of the Great Central Sun. That Heart Flame is in the Higher Mental Body, the Electronic Presence. It fills the Causal Body. It is each one's Life Stream's Eternal Perfection, Authority, and Power of Life to produce manifestation. So when you need anything constructive in the physical world, try to feel that if you desire to produce constructive manifestation, you must let the Heart Flame come forth and flow into it, in order to release the Divine Pattern by which the Perfection can be created.

In the Healing Service which We give to Life, there is always the Enfolding Heart Flame of Our Love; and as It enfolds the Life Stream of those whom We assist, the Heart Flame of each Life Stream absorbs Our Heart Flame's Love, and that becomes the Powerhouse of the individual to hold more closely to the constructive way of Life. When great Healing Power is needed for many people or individuals, there must always be some Outpouring of the Sacred Fire Love—from not only the individual's "Mighty I AM Presence," but from the Ascended Masters' Octave. Everything that mankind needs to have done in this world to bring about the Purification and the Perfection of Life must be the Flow of the Sacred Fire of Our Love into this world. Now you who move in outer world physical conditions are in the same relationship to the conditions of this world that We are to your world. Therefore, what needs to be corrected must be the Release of the Sacred Fire Love from the Great Central Sun through the Call of unascended beings.

We can love the world, and We have loved the world and wherever We have poured forth Our Love, Manifestations of Perfection have occurred and blessed Life, have been sustained, and are ever expanding their constructive action to raise all Life to greater Perfection. But each unascended person must remember that the Cosmic Law that gives the Life from the Great Central Sun into the use of the individual, expects the individual to pour forth that same Heart Flame of Love wherever manifestation occurs.

So Beloved Ones, regardless of what the world needs this hour, the only need is the Sacred Fire's Love that is the Authority and Purity and Power that just takes out of existence the discord that has been created. Mankind has densified discord

into substance so long and with such terrific hate
that no unascended being can realize how much
energy has been qualified and concentrated into
the destructive conditions of the world. But
anyone can understand Our Ascended Master
Consciousness! Everyone can understand Our
Feeling of the Sacred Fire Love that is Powerful
enough to consume human creation—consume
hate, consume discord, consume impurity—just
the same as you can take a searchlight and project it into a darkened room and do that which
you cannot do without that Light. Therefore
each of you should be an Open Door, and may
I say, a Searchlight of the Cosmic Sacred Fire
Love from the Ascended Masters' Octave to
keep pouring into this world, keep pouring into
discord everywhere, the Illumining Presence of
the Sacred Fire Love from the Ascended Masters'
Octave.

That Illumining Presence can be a Light Ray
or a Flame—or It can be the Presence of an Angel; for I assure you, the Angels of Love pour
forth that Sacred Fire Beauty, Power, and Perfection without limit with such Terrific Force that
They can silence into annihilation everything of
human creation wherever They go. Just like the

searchlight compels the darkness to cease to be
and the shadows to disappear, so can the Love
from the Healing Angels, so can the Power and
the Victory of the Angels of Sacred Fire Love
pour Their Sacred Fire into a condition. And
wherever that is poured human creation is gone.
It ceases to be! It is consumed by that Almighty
Power from the Great Central Sun. So from tonight, I trust you will feel the Presence of the
Healing Angels of Sacred Fire Love, not only in
and around yourselves when you need Them;
but call forth Their Presence into every condition
of impurity. They do not take on the impurity!
They are the Flame that moves in there the annihilation of the impurity.

This is Power Supreme, Power of which mankind does not even dream. Otherwise We could
not have performed the Miracles We have all
down through the centuries in answer to mankind's Call. We want you to feel the Presence of
the Sacred Fire Angels of such Sacred Fire Love
that even when you just think of Them and ask
Their Presence to pour that Flame of Love into
a condition to purify it, you will become aware
of Their Presence because you can *feel* Their
Presence. When you love Them, Their Love

comes back to you to make you feel It. And it's in your feeling world that this Magnificent Sacred Fire Power from the Heart of the Central Sun moves into outer physical conditions and consumes everything in its pathway that is not that Love. And oh! if mankind—if individuals would only learn what Miracles they can have, what Powers they can release, what Manifestations they can produce, what Help they can give to the rest of Life just by calling the Sacred Fire Love from the Cosmic Angels of Sacred Fire Love into those conditions—and forbid the existence of human creation!

We want so much to have you use this Power, so as We come and bring you Its Explanation, you will begin to feel the Peace which It brings inside of you. When the Angels of Sacred Fire Love begin to pour into you Their Feeling of Peace and Power and Silence of Their Hearts' Love, Their Life and Their Perfection, I assure you, you will feel It! As you continue to accept It, remember It, use It, call It into outer world conditions, It becomes a Light around you; and then you will see It. When that Light begins to come around you, you will see those Angels. There is nothing in the Ascended Masters' Oc-

tave that is any substance that can shut out Their
Presence, and when you begin to feel the Heart
Flames of the Angels of Sacred Fire Love pour
Their Feeling into you, as you feel It and love It,
accept and ask your "Beloved I AM Presence"
and Them to hold that Feeling within you forever. Their Sacred Fire Hearts' Flame of that
Love will consume the human in you just the
same as It will in outer world conditions. And
My Dear Ones, the world doesn't need anything
but that Sacred Fire Love!

Each one of the Ascended Masters—over the
many years past and in every Dictation—We have
given again and again and again the reminder to
the intellect, to the feeling, of the Magnitude of
the Power of this Fire, this Sacred Fire Love, the
Heart Flame from the Great Central Sun. You
have been reminded of the Fire Breath of the
Almighty! That is the Power of this Sacred Fire
Love that is in the very atmosphere of Earth.
And that atmosphere you must have if you are
going to live!

So if Perfection is going to live in you; if
Perfection is going to be in the world around you,
then that Heart Flame of Sacred Fire Love from
the Angels of the Sacred Fire, as well as the

Ascended Host—many of whom are those Angels—that must live in you. The Sacred Fire of the Angels of Sacred Fire Love must come into you. And as It enters into you and makes you feel Its Peace, Its Purity, and Its Love, and Its Almighty Power, that which has been an obstruction to the Perfection you desire, you will find has been dissolved and consumed. The Fulfillment of the Divine Plan begins to manifest in the physical world around you because the Life of the Angels of Sacred Fire Love has come to Earth to produce It. Once you understand how Great is this Power, you will come and dwell in the Powerhouse of Life, the Powerhouse of your "Beloved I AM Presence," the Powerhouse of the Ascended Masters' Great Temples of the Sacred Fire, all of which are the Concentration of the Sacred Fire Love from the Great Central Sun. That Love contains every Quality, every Power to produce Perfect Manifestation, make It Immortal, compel Its Expansion, protect It without limit, and send forth Its Beauty, Its Blessing, Its Power, and Its Perfection—Its Happiness and Peace for Eternity—to every particle of Life. To become that and use that Power in this world while you are yet unascended is that which We

are trying to bring to the "I AM" Student Body
for use now, because your Nation needs It!
(applause) Thank you so much, Precious Ones.
Won't you be seated, please, and just remain so.

When you think of the consuming of conditions that mankind has generated that are of
impurity and discord, as you ask always for the
consuming of the condition, fail not to ask the
Cosmic Law of Sacred Fire Love to take the
cause of those conditions out of the universe,
that they may never again touch any part of Life.
The Great Ones down through the ages—the
Angels of Healing, the Angels of Purity, the
Angels of Love and Protection—have consumed
and consumed and consumed mankind's human
creation. Now those of you who understand this
Law, by Conscious Command have full authority to demand the removal from the Earth at this
time of the cause of everything that produces
human creation.

*Your Call will enable the Cosmic Law to act more
quickly because you, as part of unascended mankind,
are the authority to demand the removal of everything
that is not the Fulfillment of the Great Divine Plan
of the Perfection for this world.* And as you call for
this in outer world conditions, you yourselves

must automatically become the Fulfillment of
that Divine Plan. Wherever you abide this Sacred
Fire Love and the Angels who pour It forth to
this world will be with you, will be the Power you
may use, will be the Guardians of that which you
are responsible for controlling. They will be your
daily Companions if you so desire! *(applause)*
Thank you so much.

When you realize how much the Great Love
of the Universe has given into manifestation;
when you realize what Courage there is within
Life; when you realize what Perfection there is
that you may bring into existence in this world,
you will understand that to consciously call forth,
feel, command, use, direct, and expand into everybody and everything you contact the Great
Central Sun's Ascended Master Heart Flame of
Sacred Fire Love—and call the Angels of Sacred
Fire Love to hold Control and Victory in everything you call forth in the physical octave—you
will find all the blessings you desire sustained.
The Divine Plan fulfilled will automatically begin to be built into this world that makes it one
day the Perfection of the Ascended Masters'
Octave. It doesn't make any difference, Dear
Ones of the Light, it doesn't make any difference

what has to be corrected in this world. The only
One, Eternal, All-Masterful Presence that is forever expanding Perfection—It must be recognized
and used and loved and called into this world,
and It is forever the Sacred Fire Love which is
the Victory of the Ascended Master Consciousness.

In the terrific experiences which were those of
the Master Jesus and Myself and those who were
with Us, if it had not been for that Sacred Fire
Love, We could never have given the Example
to the world of what it means to master the conditions of the physical octave and to overcome
mankind's hatred. The more mankind generates
discord, the more must those who understand
this Law call forth the Sacred Fire Love that is
such Terrific Power of Immortal Purity, that as
you demand It go into conditions that are destructive, demand without limit the Great Central
Sun's Legions of the Angels of Sacred Fire Love
that move into the physical conditions of this
world that which, if need be, can silence on the
instant everything of human discord. And I assure you, when those Beings of the Sacred Fire
Love who have never yet been embodied in the
physical body—those Beings are created by the

Great Beings in the Great Central Sun especially to handle the Concentration of this Sacred Fire Love in Cosmic Power that affects the whole system of worlds—and when They appear and that Power goes forth, nothing else can exist!

That is the Help We are offering you tonight! That is the Power We ask you to use to offset mankind's continual creation of impurity, discord, and hatred. Beloved Ones, the Powerhouse has been opened to your use! The Door is wide open into the Ascended Masters' Octave! There are no more obstructions to those who know this Law. All We ask you to do is to use It now in outer physical conditions as powerfully as you can, that you may have that same Blessing within yourselves as you call It into physical conditions to prevent what the sinister force intends.

As you enter into the continual use of this, We will not need to say anything more. Your own experiences will prove to you the Joy it is to call It into this octave to correct the conditions that all mankind together cannot correct. Nothing can do away with mankind's frightful creation of evil except the Angels of that Sacred Fire Love from the Great Central Sun whose Power is without limit. Concentration of that Sacred Fire from

Their own Blazing Hearts can forever handle everything mankind has created of discord. And yet They never enter into it! The Flame goes ahead, and nothing else can exist but Its Presence.

When you want Power without limit to handle physical conditions that are vicious, call forth the Legions of the Angels of Sacred Fire Love to reveal and use and show Their Power of Control of physical destructive conditions. When you call forth the Legions from the Great Central Sun of the Angels of Sacred Fire Love in such Overwhelming Power human creation cannot exist, be prepared to see the change take place that will awaken many of those at this time who are caught in the clutches of destructive forces, but who have Light enough to be made to turn to the constructive way of Life at this time. This is the Purpose of My coming tonight, that I may bring Freedom to those Life Streams who have been caught in the toils of destructive forces, and yet who know well enough that destructive conditions cannot succeed!

You can be part of the Legions of Freedom to those Life Streams as well as Us. We can pour forth the Sacred Fire through you. Be unconcerned! Just call the Great Central Sun's Legions of the Angels of Sacred Fire Love to pour Their Power without limit into those Life Streams and force the awakening that takes them out of the clutches of the sinister force. There will be many, many, many Life Streams at this time that can be turned to the Light and that will bless you for-ever, because you were the Strength of the Light that drew them out of the shadows and into the Sacred Fire's Love that is Immortal Freedom.

This is the Freedom of your Beloved Saint Germain, because the Violet Consuming Flame's Sacred Fire Love can be of such intensity the human cannot exist. Beloved Ones, We have healed and healed and healed, but mankind needs to be healed with the Illumination that makes the individual within feel that he or she does not want to any longer create the shadows. It is to awaken these Life Streams from within, and allow the Desire from within to come into outer world conditions, and command that destructive forces shall forever cease existence.

When you know how many Healing Angels have enfolded mankind down through the ages, down through the centuries throughout the world wherever Healing has taken place, you must realize that from an Ascended Master's

standpoint, that must someday come into the use
of unascended beings; for they must be taught
to use this Power to free the rest of humanity.
And as that takes place, automatically you free
yourselves!

So the Healing Angels are the Angels of Freedom! The Healing Flame is the Sacred Fire
Love! When you ask the Legions of the Healing
Angels, the Angels of Sacred Fire Love, to clothe
you in Their Miracle Mantle of the Cosmic
Love's Prevention of human creation wherever
you abide—just as certainly as you make the
Call—will you find the Fulfillment of that Call
becoming a part of your own Life Stream. So
may you go forward and live in the Heart Realm
of Life. I shall ever be close to you; for no part
of Life can call to Me for Sacred Fire Love that
I do not respond; for I will always respond, and
with more than the individual knows exists. It is
Our Privilege, Our Way of Life, Our Divine Plan
fulfilled that offers the Sacred Fire Love of Immortal Mastery over this world. Then Peace
becomes Eternal, and you become the Manifestation of It and have the right and authority to
command It to control conditions around you—
and you are no longer subject to the discordant

conditions that heretofore you have felt you could not overcome. You can overcome everything with this Power of the Sacred Fire Love, and the Angels of the Sacred Fire Love are the Guardians of all who want the constructive way of Life.

So We leave you enfolded in the Great Cosmic Miracle Mantle of Eternal Power, the Sacred Fire Love and Healing Peace, and the Almighty Victory and Full Ascended Master Control of Manifestation by that Sacred Fire Love that forever floods everything with Greater and Greater Perfection, and is Master for Eternity! I commend you to that Heart Flame, and may It forever teach you of all that is in the Ascended Masters' Octave till you come to Us for Eternity. Thank you with all My Heart.

CHAPTER XVII

BELOVED ANGEL DEVA OF THE JADE TEMPLE

Chicago, Illinois
August 11, 1966
Record CD 1244

Beloved Ones of the Mighty Saint Germain's Family, I trust I may bring to you tonight an understanding of some of the Activities that the Ascended Host are constantly pouring forth to enable that which is constructive to be protected and continue its blessing to mankind. Whenever a work of any kind is to be accomplished and something constructive drawn forth into outer manifestation, before that can be done, there must always be one or more of the Angelic Host who provide a Focus of the Violet Consuming Flame and the Sacred Fire's Love into the physical octave to be the Guard of the locality, and Guard of the atmosphere in which the manifestation is to be drawn.

Now just as you have insulation on the wires of your electrical apparatus, and that confines, so to speak, or separates the electricity within the wire from the static electricity in the atmosphere so you can use it in concentrated action; just so do We, from the Inner standpoint, draw forth certain Activities of the Sacred Fire into the outer physical conditions that surround mankind. And then after that Focus of the Sacred Fire is concentrated and held protected for a certain length of time—held sustained—then into that does there descend the direction and the form, the concentration of the energy, the substance, the consciousness, and the design of what is to be brought into manifestation in the physical world.

Now this has gone on through the ages, and everything that you have of modern civilization that is a convenience for you today, that you use just so naturally, has had to have the Protection of the Angelic Host before it could be brought into manifestation. If you could have seen at the Inner level what had to take place before the railroads were brought forth, before the steamboats were constructed and drawn forth over the last century or two, if you could have seen at the Inner level what has to be done in preparation for some marvelous constructive blessing to be brought into the physical world for mankind to use, you would be utterly amazed. But nevertheless, the Cosmic Law is not only wise, It is always constructive; and It is always a Blessing to Life, and It is always the Release of Greater Happiness.

So when you want to be happy, when you're thinking of your own happiness or that of others, try to realize, when you want to do something constructive, that if you will remember what the Great Divine Plan is for the manifestation of something constructive, you can set into action these various Activities of the Sacred Fire to be the Guard of that which you wish to produce to bless someone else or to give its blessing to the world.

If mankind but understood how the Ascended Host create a planet and the magnificent blessings and manifestations that are drawn into existence for mankind's use, if mankind understood this, there could be a very much greater release of the blessings which mankind creates in the continual use of energy, which is the Law of Action in this world. You might wonder sometimes why mankind is kept so busy doing something all the time. If that were not accomplished, if mankind, individuals everywhere were not allowed to use the energy of Life in constructive activity and creation of that which brings—sometimes brings enjoyment, sometimes does not—it would be impossible for mankind to exist, and action go on in order to hold constructive activities protected.

If it were not necessary for individuals to create something that is constructive and continually use the energy of Life and the consciousness to create something constructive, you not only would have inertia, you would eventually have the return to the second death, because when the creative activities of Life—through the mind, and the Love of the Heart Flame—when they're not allowed to go forth and fulfill the Divine Plan and reveal Its Magnificent Blessings and Perfection, well then, it has to return to the universal.

When the Mighty Saint Germain decided to bring forth this Instruction of the "Mighty I AM Presence," I took the responsibility of providing the atmosphere, purifying the atmosphere, and holding concentrated a certain amount of the Sacred Fire within this city, into which He drew that which He wanted to give as the Illumination and Instruction of the "Beloved Mighty I AM Presence," in order to draw into that Sacred Fire the Life Streams who were to accept this Teaching of the "Mighty I AM Presence," who were to receive the Light Rays that He and others of the Ascended Host have poured forth into those who have come into the "I AM" Activity to understand the Law and use Its Power. This has gone on constantly, and therefore everything He wishes to give is at all times surrounded by and insulated by some Cosmic Activities of the Sacred Fire and the Cosmic Light Substance. This is the Great Natural Law of Creation, and the producing of manifestation that is to build a civilization or produce Perfection on a planet until it one day becomes a Focus for the Power of the Sacred Fire's Love that produces a Sun.

This same thing goes on in the Creation and Activities of the Powers of Nature. When the Mighty Lord the Maha Chohan chooses to produce a Manifestation through the Powers of Nature to give mankind a Greater Blessing, there must come always first those Angels who draw certain Activities of the Sacred Fire into balanced action, hold Them concentrated and sustained, until the Lord the Maha Chohan designs and

lowers into that the Substance, and the Divine
Pattern that fulfills the Plan that He has to produce the Manifestation that blesses the Powers of
Nature, and blesses mankind through the Powers
of Nature.

Therefore, no matter what it is that you wish
to do in the physical world—so long as it be constructive—if you will just set the habit of, first of
all, calling to your "Beloved I AM Presence" and
the Ascended Host to blaze in and around you
the Ascended Masters' Fiery Christ Truth of
what you need to know to produce Perfection,
and the Fiery Christ Protecting Sacred Fire that
is necessary to be the Guard before you produce
what you want to in outer manifestation, you
would never have problems. You would never
have failure. You would never have anything that
would be discordant.

So it is to help you come to this use of the
Great Powers of Life, that tonight it is My
Privilege to enfold each of you and the Mighty
Saint Germain's "I AM" Activities everywhere in
the world in the added Concentration of the
Sacred Fire of Our Love for the Greater Pro-
tection of all that is constructive, and to bring
through the Inspiration of the "Mighty I AM

Presence" and the Ascended Host the Greater
Blessings from the Ascended Masters' Octave.

Now We are constantly lowering those into
outer use if mankind would only recognize
where this Perfection comes from, and what it
is necessary to do to hold Protection around
everything that is constructive; so that which is
still remaining of discord in the outer world
cannot interfere with that Perfection, and cannot
destroy the constructive activities that are
released for the Fulfillment of the Great Divine
Plan.

In all use of consciousness and energy and the
feeling world, there must come first always the
Heart Flame of Love. And when individuals understand this and will use It before you start
anything in the physical world that is constructive activity, if you will always provide the Focus
of the Sacred Fire's Purifying, All-protecting
Love in the locality where you're going to produce something constructive, and then demand
that that be eternally sustained, whatever you do
that fulfills the Great Divine Plan will come forth
Perfect. And then you of your own free will can
call for that Perfection which you create to be
made Imperishable and Self-luminous, and to

be made an Eternal Blessing, not only to you, but to every particle of Life that contacts It.

When the Mighty God Tabor created the magnificent Beauty and Perfection that is within His Retreat, His Love, His Sacred Fire Power, has enfolded that from the beginning, and still is Its Guard. And it is His Sacred Fire Love that has prevented any human being ever beholding It till He gets ready to show It! Now that's what it means to understand the Great Creative Activities of Life, cooperate with Them, and want to fulfill the Great Divine Plan.

So Blessed Ones, if I may be of Help to you in this respect, whatever you wish to do that is constructive, stop, first of all, and call for the Fiery Christ Truth of the Ascended Masters' Way to do it, and all that you need to know to produce Perfection that is Eternal. And then call for the Enfolding Sacred Fire Love from the Jade Temple to be the Eternal Purity which is a Protection that keeps it insulated against destructive forces. This is how that which has blessed mankind down through the ages has been sustained, even in the midst of mankind's destruction. And the same thing is true of you— of individuals.

So now if you'll just set the habit before you do anything, of just calling for what your "Mighty I AM Presence" knows you need to know, and what the Angelic Host can give you to protect what you're going to do before you do it, you will never know failure. And as this becomes a habit, you will find no more problems. So this is part of the Answer to the Call you made tonight. *(applause)* Thank you so much, Precious Ones. Won't you be seated please. Just remain so. There are so many magnificent Blessings and such Happiness could come to mankind if individuals would understand this and use It!

Therefore, in the Great Creative Activities of the Universe, you—all of you—need to know and remember that there are the Temples of the Sacred Fire in the Ascended Masters' Octave from which the Sacred Fire in Unlimited Power can be concentrated and drawn into any condition in the physical octave to create and to sustain that which is constructive. We hope when the Earth is purified and mankind purified—awakened and purified and illumined—We hope to show you a replica in the physical octave of some of these Temples of the Sacred Fire. And if you ever behold Them, you will realize how crude has been even the best of mankind's construction of buildings and architectural design in the physical world.

We want to perfect this world. We can only perfect it through the humanity who are privileged to embody here, and We can only perfect it by bringing the Perfection of Our Octave into this world. But before It can come, there must come this Sacred Fire Concentration of the Sacred Fire's Eternal Purity in order to protect the Concentration of the Power and the Substance by which the Magnificent Perfection can be drawn into this world for mankind to use, to enjoy, to bless all Life, and to raise all into the Victory of the Ascension.

So Blessed Ones, no matter what changes take place in the outer world, the chaos of the outer world is due to filth. If you want the constructive activities of Life, then there must come within you the Sacred Fire's Eternal Purity, the Sacred Fire's Consciousness of the Ascended Masters' Octave, and the Sacred Fire's Power that you use in physical conditions to produce that which as yet mankind cannot and has not produced. There are ways and means of creating Perfection into this world by the use of the Powers of the Sacred

Fire which are used in the Ascended Masters' Octave—that of which mankind knows absolutely nothing. And I can assure you, anything that comes from the Ascended Masters' Octave is not terribly complicated. Everything of Perfection is simple and balanced and imperishable and Self-luminous.

Whatever you wish to do in the physical world, if you will stop first and demand the Ascended Masters' Indestructible Purity and the Sacred Fire's Indestructible Purifying Love to concentrate into the energy you're going to use; and demand that that Purity repel and consume everything that is the discord and impurity of mankind in the atmosphere, you would go forward; and you could build something constructive—successfully, happily, invincibly. And then someone in the outer world could not take it away from you or distort it or destroy it or desecrate it. This is Eternal Protection against everything in mankind that is destructive.

So when it becomes necessary in order to bring Greater Illumination to the consciousness of the people of this world, I'm sure you realize, there must come first the Release of the Sacred Fire's Greater Purity and Purifying Love, in order to provide the Protection for the Greater Light and the Greater Consciousness to come into the individuals who embody in this world. So when you wish to fill yourselves with the Ascended Masters' Perfection, begin always with the Purifying Love of the Violet Consuming Flame, your Love, Wisdom and Power in Perfect Balance of the Unfed Flame; and then as the Sevenfold Flame of the Seven Mighty Elohim is drawn in and around you, It holds Protection and supplies the various Powers and Activities of the Sacred Fire that enable you to create something constructive.

The Seven Mighty Elohim must be recognized, because They are referred to in your Bible as the Seven Builders around the Throne; and They are concerned with every bit of constructive activity on this Earth that mankind has ever used down through the ages, or ever will. They are the Beings who release the Powers, the Intelligence, the Illumination and the Consciousness and the Sacred Fire Love that enables constructive activity to be drawn into the physical world to create something wonderful to bless mankind. It is the Divine Way to live Life, and It does not contain problems! And certainly the consciousness of mankind should be consumed that has constantly accepted that the Great "God Presence" of Life at any time designs anything through the discord and evil mankind has generated.

I want you to feel tonight that there is the Enfolding, Blazing Sacred Fire Protection of Our Love that will always guard you—if you'll call It into action and guard anything constructive that you want to do. This is part of Our Service to Life. It is Our Way of protecting what is constructive so It can become Eternal. Therefore in the opportunities that lie ahead of you to help design the Incoming Golden Age, you will be very privileged, and I am sure very happy, to draw forth from the Ascended Masters' Octave the things that We know this world is going to need in order to give mankind the opportunity to understand and use these Master Powers of Life and produce what is to be a Blessing here for Eternity. And in the right use of all Activities of the Sacred Fire, the Cosmic Light Substance and the Energy of this Universe—by the right Consciousness, you automatically raise yourselves into the Greater Perfection that one day is your Ascension.

The same thing must take place for the Earth. There must come the Purity into the physical structure of Earth and into the Powers of Nature and Forces of the Elements that forever manifests the Beauty and the Perfection and the Joy of the Love of the Sacred Fire, to raise the Earth and all upon it into Our Octave of Perfection, wherein the Ever-expanding Glory and Happiness of every bit of Love of the Sacred Fire goes on and gives Itself to the Universe around you to forever expand your Happiness.

People in this world seek Happiness, and it's here today and gone tomorrow, or gone the next second, because they know naught where it is. They know naught how to create it. They do not know what Ascended Master Happiness is. So if you come to the time when you want happiness, remember, if it is to be sustained, if it is to be Eternal, it must begin with some Activity of the Sacred Fire Love from the Ascended Masters' Octave.

Now your "Beloved I AM Presence" would be the Builder through you, but your "Beloved I AM Presence," in Its Release through you of Its own Life, is guarded by the Seven Mighty Elohim of Creation, guarded by the Sevenfold Flame in your forehead, guarded by the Love from the Ascended Masters' Octave that is your Protecting Presence until you can create that which is constructive and fulfills the Great Divine Plan.

I could go on indefinitely in the Explanation of this, but I give you just enough tonight to show you how you can, in anything you want to do, so long as it be constructive, if you will, start with your Call to your "Beloved I AM Presence" to tell you the Ascended Masters' Fiery Christ Truth of what you need to know to produce the Perfection you desire. And then you call to the Seven Mighty Elohim and the Angelic Host, and those who govern the creation of Perfection in Manifestation to come and hold the Sacred Fire Love of Eternal Protection around that which you wish to do until it is completed, and your Victory is attained. And your Joy will know no bounds, and everything you do will be successful. Everything you do to help others will be successful, because there is nothing to interfere then with the Perfection that the "Mighty I AM Presence" is lowering into your outer use. And there's nothing but Perfection can come to you from the Ascended Masters and Cosmic Beings, or the use of the Sacred Fire and the Cosmic Light.

It is this Consciousness mankind needs. What think you, with the Magnificent Blessings there are in this world, that a mankind—a whole group of human beings—can use the energy and consciousness of Life to destroy and desecrate and hurt some other part of Life? How could that be the Divine Plan? It isn't, never was, and never will be! So Blessed Ones, this is Our Way of living the Eternal, Divine Perfection of Life. It is the Eternal Divine Plan fulfilled, and It forever gives Its Blessing to everything in the Universe! And no thing can come back to the individual but more Blessing. This is the only way mankind will ever be free from destructive forces and destructive conditions and destructive consciousness that has engulfed mankind, and would destroy everything except for the Love and the Sacred Fire that is drawn into outer manifestation by the Ascended Host and the Angelic Host. And I can assure you, if you continue with your Calls to the Angel Legions of the Victorious Cosmic Christ, or the Angel Legions of the Violet Flame, or any Activity of the Sacred Fire you call, if you continue your Calls to Them, you will find Them giving you every possible Assistance. And the more They surround you, the less human beings and human creation can come near you to interfere with that which you wish to accomplish.

So if you want success, if you want your Victory of the Ascension, if you want to do that which is constructive to help the rest of life, then the Angelic Host must become not only your Partners, but They must become your Protectors. For while you are busy creating something here, They stand the Guard with the Sacred Fire that keeps away everything that would disturb you.

And it is very practical to live with Them. It's no figment of anybody's imagination! There are those of the Angelic Host who have never been in physical embodiment, but They are created to hold Their Flame of Love around anything and everything that is constructive in order to let It fulfill the Great Divine Plan. Part of the Angelic Host are Ascended, and part of Them are not; the Ones who are not have never been in physical embodiment. Those who are Ascended have passed this way.

There is no such thing as failure! And I again will say, as did your Beloved Saint Germain and others of the Ascended Host: There is no such thing as a fallen Angel. The Angelic Host are either Ascended Beings, or They are Beings of the Sacred Fire that have never been in the physical world. So how can They fall? Don't you see how confused mankind has become—what lies have been imposed upon Life because they would not use the Sacred Fire's Purifying Love to protect that which needs to be accomplished in the physical world! But you do not need to be a part of the discord of mankind's mistakes of the past—your own, or anyone else's.

When you say to your "Presence": "Release me from every mistake I've ever made, and replace those mistakes by such Ascended Master Sacred Fire Blessing and Perfection and Happiness to the rest of Life that I never think of them again! They never can be existing anywhere in the universe, and no one else can be touched by them."

You can forgive your own mistakes—you must! And Forgiveness means to give the Love and the Sacred Fire's Perfection into a condition to consume what is wrong and reveal the Perfection of that which is right and protect It until the Great Divine Plan can bless all for Eternity. And if that isn't the Divine Way to live life, then what could be? And certainly mankind needs to learn how to live the Divine Way of Life!

There have been plenty of Divine Blessings placed in this world to help mankind gain the Ascension. But since We are interested in *you*, and I was interested in Beloved Saint Germain's Mighty Effort to purify the Earth and bring forth this Cosmic Illumination and Fiery Christ Truth of the "Mighty I AM Presence," then I am still interested in helping you to be cut free from, and insulated from the discord that otherwise brings failure and problems and distress and limitation. So if you care to remember that My Love and My Sacred Fire has enfolded His Mighty Work, I can enfold yours, too. *(applause)* Thank you so much.

There's one more thing. It is a known fact in some channels—not all—that jade, what you call physical jade in the substance and structure of this Earth, does not take on the discordant radiation of any human being or condition of discord in this world. It's Eternally Pure. Some substance takes on the radiation of mankind's discord, and some other substance does not. Gold is Eternally Pure, and Jade is Eternally Pure. Therefore It is a Protection within certain conditions that keeps the discord and destruction away from that which is being accomplished, or being built, to produce the Fulfillment of the Divine Plan.

So there are many things that will be a blessing to you as you learn them, and then begin to use them to help the Great Cosmic Scheme of Creation build and build and build the Perfection that the Divine Plan intends for life, that It may only create Happiness. Did you know the Divine Plan is only to create Happiness? So when people want Happiness, why don't they turn to the Source of Happiness? This world hasn't given It. And what the majority of people call happiness is temporary sensation—has nothing whatsoever to do with Eternal Happiness. Eternal Happiness is not just temporary sensation. Eternal Happiness is a Magnificent Mastery of Life that is the Controller of all substance, all energy, and all consciousness anywhere in Infinite Space, that always produces Perfection—and always, through that Perfection, gives Happiness to some other part of Life. And truly, that is the Divine Plan, and certainly, It should be fulfilled.

So Blessed Ones, I, too, have a Mantle, a Miracle Mantle of Love's Happiness! And if you should by any chance care to wear It or experiment with It, I can show you some very delightful things that just as certainly as you exist will

t, it will give Us the opening to draw into the
ical conditions by which you are surrounded
Activities of the Sacred Fire, because the
lic Host are the Directors of that Sacred
Those who are Ascended in the Angelic
re those who concentrate It and direct It
rious places on the Earth's surface to con-
s rapidly as possible the impurity and
nankind has generated.

We draw your attention to the Activi-
Angelic Host or the Ascended Host or
c Beings, it is always because We want
thing extra through you to bless you,
ou, and to help you become Victori-
now, the more you recognize the
ible Presence of the Angelic Host
closer We can come. The closer We
e We pour the Feeling of Our own
into your emotional bodies. There
ification must take place, and the
chored within and around your
s to keep repelled from you the
in the atmosphere in which you
en We come to offer you Our
We come to offer you Protec-
ver the hordes of evil.

bless you for Eternity, because the Eternal Purity
of the Jade Temple, it seems to Me, is needed
very much in this world this hour. So Blessed
Ones, My Miracle Mantle of Love's Mastery is,
I assure you, a very Powerful, Wonderful Blessing, and is a very practical Way and Means of
protecting you and that which you wish to accomplish. So I offer It to you to help the Beloved
Saint Germain in the gigantic task He has accepted of purifying this Earth and all upon It.
Only the Ascended Host and Cosmic Beings
have any comprehension of what that means. But
you can help Him, and when you begin to see
that take place and mankind's human creation be
consumed, your Joy will know no bounds and
will know no end.

I offer you the Happiness of Eternity, the
Magnificent, Invincible Mastery of Life, and the
Victorious, Joyous Use of everything—substance,
energy, consciousness, manifestation—everything
in existence, to build that Perfection which is
Eternal and forever expanding. So I leave you
to the enjoyment of understanding this Law,
using It, and making yourselves a channel by
which Its Great Perfection can come to the rest
of Life as well as to you. And your Happiness

in making others happy will forever be expanding and Invincible. I commend you to your
Freedom. Thank you with all My Heart.

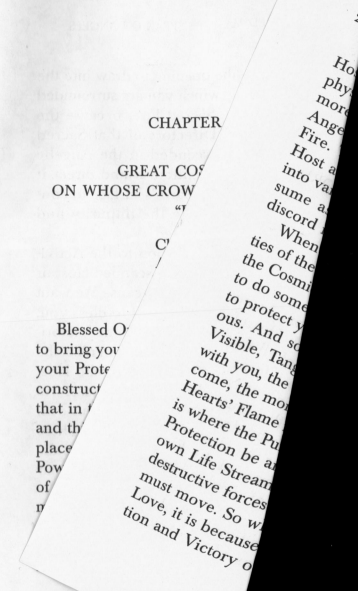

The more you can recognize the Angels of the Sacred Fire and ask Their Presence with you to abide with you—and you accept Their Presence with you, and you call Their Sacred Fire into every condition with which you come in contact to demand the Purification that sets the Earth Free—We can release Unlimited Power. That is what you have been calling forth when you call forth the Master Power Presence of the Sacred Fire. But It must be concentrated and directed by Intelligent Beings who are Its Master, and that is what the Angelic Host are.

So if you will accept Our Nearness to you, We can come closer and closer into the outer activities of mankind and release more Power to consume the evil that has been generated by mankind's frightful hate and wars and the desecration in the misuse of Life. When We come and offer Our Help to you, it is always the Sacred Fire Purifying Love of Our Life Streams to come in and around you and hold enough Purity within and around you to be your Protection; for I assure you, there is no Protection for destructive forces. We cannot—We do not—the Sacred Fire never will protect that which is evil. So if you will dwell with Us, We will dwell with you! The more you think of Us, the more of Our Sacred Fire from Our Ascended Master Octave We can anchor in and around you as an Eternal Sun Presence from Our Ascended Master Octave that becomes One with your Life Stream forever. Therefore, in recognizing Our Presence, recognize the Sacred Fire that comes with Us to accomplish what is necessary to dispose of the hordes of evil—whether they be within and around you or in the atmosphere or conditions in which you move in the outer world; or whether they affect the city or the nation or the atmosphere of Earth or anybody or anything in the rest of the world.

In the Great Cleansing Process that must take place everywhere throughout this city and the nation and the world, there is only one Power that's going to do it, and that is the Sacred Fire which the Angelic Host direct and sustain and control. So when you want physical conditions to be controlled by that which is constructive, then flood those conditions with the Angelic Host's Sacred Fire of whatever Power controls them. If you'll understand this tonight, you can start your Momentum by your constant recognition of the Angelic Host's Legions of the Sacred Fire that overwhelm and control everything that is destructive in this world; if mankind will only reach up and call It into action, so We may focus It into the physical conditions that you need. But if people ignore Us and will not accept this and will not do what is necessary to open the way for Us to release the Sacred Fire, they will stay in their chains until they do.

How do you feel when you offer someone help and it is refused? Are you to blame then for what happens to the person whom you're trying to help? We have offered and offered and offered! And every time any Ascended Master offers you Help—any of the Angelic Host, any of the Cosmic Beings—It is always the Sacred Fire of Our Love. And Our Love is Eternal Purity! Our Love is Indestructible Power! Our Love is Eternal Protection! Why mankind won't reach up and accept It and call It into action and let Us anchor It and concentrate It to remove these conditions shows you just how enfolded mankind is in the destructive forces of its own selfishness!

Therefore when We plead and plead with people, and offer and offer these Activities of the Sacred Fire that are Master over everything in this world, mankind must awaken to the fact that it is Our Purifying Love and Our Power of Life that must come into these conditions if evil is to be conquered, if evil is to be annihilated, if evil is to be prevented from desecrating any more Life in this world. So the very survival of mankind on this Earth is dependent upon the Angelic Host!

When mankind, century after century, has destroyed and destroyed and destroyed the many Gifts that the Great Law of Life has permitted to become manifest in this world, and then becomes enslaved to the creation of selfishness and destruction, you can see how dead asleep is the consciousness of the mankind of this world who will not reach up and accept the Help We've offered—because from the beginning of mankind's embodiment on this Earth, human beings in this world have been told repeatedly, age after age after age in every cycle, "Call unto Me, and I will answer thee." So now you are either going to have the Miracles of Our Sacred Fire Protecting Love or you won't have the Protection! When I made that Statement, *"If necessary, the Light of a Thousand Suns shall descend into the Earth, and dissolve and consume all human selfishness!"*—that hour is now! You need It! And mankind won't wake up and call for It; then you are helpless before the destructive forces the people of this world have generated through one war after another!

So tonight I come to bring you release and relief, and to rescue you—if you care to accept Our Presence with you. *(applause)* Thank you so much. Won't you be seated, please, and just remain so. Mankind's ingratitude for the Love and the Blessings We have poured to this world—which most of human beings take for granted—is the thing that has prevented the Illumination coming to the intellect by which the individual could hold to the constructive way of Life long enough to gain the Freedom and Victory of the Ascension. But what think you is the Action of the Cosmic Law when We who stand ready to consume mankind's frightful human creation, the frightful evil forces that are on this Earth; and We beg and beg and beg people to accept Our Love and the Reality of Our Presence with them, and ask them to call Us into action so We can set you Free, and then mankind does not respond? What think you is the Action of the Cosmic Law?

Mankind does not need to suffer unless it so chooses. The discord and the filth and the destruction generated by mankind through one war after another has reached a momentum that would destroy the Earth itself if it were not for the Love of the Higher Mental Body of each Life Stream and the Love of the Ascended Host. And when that Love is the Sacred Fire before which every destructive force must be dissolved and consumed—and harmoniously, without suffering—We have offered and offered and offered, and now if the Cosmic Fiat has to go forth to shock mankind awake by the activities of Nature of which We are Master, the human beings of this world will want some Assistance!

Blessed Ones, We come to offer you Our Love! We have offered you the Sacred Fire! Whenever you think of the Sacred Fire, remember also to remind yourself, It is the Purifying Love of either the "Mighty I AM Presence" or the Ascended Host. The Angelic Host are the Beings who concentrate It, who call It forth from the Physical Sun and the Great Central Sun. We call It forth from Our Temples of the Sacred Fire in the Ascended Masters' Octave. Those Temples of the Sacred Fire are the Cosmic Concentration and Momentum of Our Life's Love that We have used down through the ages bless you for Eternity, because the Eternal Purity of the Jade Temple, it seems to Me, is needed very much in this world this hour. So Blessed Ones, My Miracle Mantle of Love's Mastery is, I assure you, a very Powerful, Wonderful Blessing, and is a very practical Way and Means of protecting you and that which you wish to accomplish. So I offer It to you to help the Beloved Saint Germain in the gigantic task He has accepted of purifying this Earth and all upon It. Only the Ascended Host and Cosmic Beings have any comprehension of what that means. But you can help Him, and when you begin to see that take place and mankind's human creation be consumed, your Joy will know no bounds and will know no end.

I offer you the Happiness of Eternity, the Magnificent, Invincible Mastery of Life, and the Victorious, Joyous Use of everything—substance, energy, consciousness, manifestation—everything in existence, to build that Perfection which is Eternal and forever expanding. So I leave you to the enjoyment of understanding this Law, using It, and making yourselves a channel by which Its Great Perfection can come to the rest of Life as well as to you. And your Happiness in making others happy will forever be expanding and Invincible. I commend you to your Freedom. Thank you with all My Heart.

CHAPTER XVIII

GREAT COSMIC ANGEL
ON WHOSE CROWN BLAZES THE WORD
"UNION"

Chicago, Illinois
August 12, 1966
Record CD 1245

Blessed Ones of the Heart of Freedom, I come to bring you this night the Power of My Heart for your Protection and the Protection of all that is constructive everywhere. I wish to inform you that in the handling of conditions in this Nation and this world, in the Purification that must take place, the Angelic Host are those who draw that Power into the physical world for the cleansing of the Powers of Nature and Forces of the Elements—as well as the cleansing of mankind and the atmosphere itself.

So as you give more recognition to the Limitless, Unconquerable Legions of the Angelic

Host, it will give Us the opening to draw into the physical conditions by which you are surrounded more Activities of the Sacred Fire, because the Angelic Host are the Directors of that Sacred Fire. Those who are Ascended in the Angelic Host are those who concentrate It and direct It into various places on the Earth's surface to consume as rapidly as possible the impurity and discord mankind has generated.

When We draw your attention to the Activities of the Angelic Host or the Ascended Host or the Cosmic Beings, it is always because We want to do something extra through you to bless you, to protect you, and to help you become Victorious. And so now, the more you recognize the Visible, Tangible Presence of the Angelic Host with you, the closer We can come. The closer We come, the more We pour the Feeling of Our own Hearts' Flame into your emotional bodies. There is where the Purification must take place, and the Protection be anchored within and around your own Life Streams to keep repelled from you the destructive forces in the atmosphere in which you must move. So when We come to offer you Our Love, it is because We come to offer you Protection and Victory over the hordes of evil.

The more you can recognize the Angels of the Sacred Fire and ask Their Presence with you to abide with you—and you accept Their Presence with you, and you call Their Sacred Fire into every condition with which you come in contact to demand the Purification that sets the Earth Free—We can release Unlimited Power. That is what you have been calling forth when you call forth the Master Power Presence of the Sacred Fire. But It must be concentrated and directed by Intelligent Beings who are Its Master, and that is what the Angelic Host are.

So if you will accept Our Nearness to you, We can come closer and closer into the outer activities of mankind and release more Power to consume the evil that has been generated by mankind's frightful hate and wars and the desecration in the misuse of Life. When We come and offer Our Help to you, it is always the Sacred Fire Purifying Love of Our Life Streams to come in and around you and hold enough Purity within and around you to be your Protection; for I assure you, there is no Protection for destructive forces. We cannot—We do not—the Sacred Fire never will protect that which is evil. So if you will dwell with Us, We will dwell

with you! The more you think of Us, the more
of Our Sacred Fire from Our Ascended Master
Octave We can anchor in and around you as an
Eternal Sun Presence from Our Ascended Master
Octave that becomes One with your Life Stream
forever. Therefore, in recognizing Our Presence,
recognize the Sacred Fire that comes with Us to
accomplish what is necessary to dispose of the
hordes of evil—whether they be within and
around you or in the atmosphere or conditions
in which you move in the outer world; or
whether they affect the city or the nation or the
atmosphere of Earth or anybody or anything in
the rest of the world.

In the Great Cleansing Process that must take
place everywhere throughout this city and the
nation and the world, there is only one Power
that's going to do it, and that is the Sacred Fire
which the Angelic Host direct and sustain and
control. So when you want physical conditions to
be controlled by that which is constructive, then
flood those conditions with the Angelic Host's
Sacred Fire of whatever Power controls them. If
you'll understand this tonight, you can start your
Momentum by your constant recognition of the
Angelic Host's Legions of the Sacred Fire that

overwhelm and control everything that is destructive in this world; if mankind will only
reach up and call It into action, so We may focus
It into the physical conditions that you need. But
if people ignore Us and will not accept this and
will not do what is necessary to open the way for
Us to release the Sacred Fire, they will stay in
their chains until they do.

How do you feel when you offer someone
help and it is refused? Are you to blame then for
what happens to the person whom you're trying
to help? We have offered and offered and offered! And every time any Ascended Master
offers you Help—any of the Angelic Host, any of
the Cosmic Beings—It is always the Sacred Fire
of Our Love. And Our Love is Eternal Purity!
Our Love is Indestructible Power! Our Love is
Eternal Protection! Why mankind won't reach up
and accept It and call It into action and let Us
anchor It and concentrate It to remove these
conditions shows you just how enfolded mankind
is in the destructive forces of its own selfishness!

Therefore when We plead and plead with
people, and offer and offer these Activities of the
Sacred Fire that are Master over everything in
this world, mankind must awaken to the fact that

it is Our Purifying Love and Our Power of Life that must come into these conditions if evil is to be conquered, if evil is to be annihilated, if evil is to be prevented from desecrating any more Life in this world. So the very survival of mankind on this Earth is dependent upon the Angelic Host!

When mankind, century after century, has destroyed and destroyed and destroyed the many Gifts that the Great Law of Life has permitted to become manifest in this world, and then becomes enslaved to the creation of selfishness and destruction, you can see how dead asleep is the consciousness of the mankind of this world who will not reach up and accept the Help We've offered—because from the beginning of mankind's embodiment on this Earth, human beings in this world have been told repeatedly, age after age after age in every cycle, "Call unto Me, and I will answer thee." So now you are either going to have the Miracles of Our Sacred Fire Protecting Love or you won't have the Protection! When I made that Statement, *"If necessary, the Light of a Thousand Suns shall descend into the Earth, and dissolve and consume all human selfishness!"*—that hour is now! You need It! And mankind won't wake up and call for It; then you are helpless before the destructive forces the people of this world have generated through one war after another!

So tonight I come to bring you release and relief, and to rescue you—if you care to accept Our Presence with you. *(applause)* Thank you so much. Won't you be seated, please, and just remain so. Mankind's ingratitude for the Love and the Blessings We have poured to this world—which most of human beings take for granted—is the thing that has prevented the Illumination coming to the intellect by which the individual could hold to the constructive way of Life long enough to gain the Freedom and Victory of the Ascension. But what think you is the Action of the Cosmic Law when We who stand ready to consume mankind's frightful human creation, the frightful evil forces that are on this Earth; and We beg and beg and beg people to accept Our Love and the Reality of Our Presence with them, and ask them to call Us into action so We can set you Free, and then mankind does not respond? What think you is the Action of the Cosmic Law?

Mankind does not need to suffer unless it so chooses. The discord and the filth and the destruction generated by mankind through one war after another has reached a momentum that would destroy the Earth itself if it were not for the Love of the Higher Mental Body of each Life Stream and the Love of the Ascended Host. And when that Love is the Sacred Fire before which every destructive force must be dissolved and consumed—and harmoniously, without suffering—We have offered and offered and offered, and now if the Cosmic Fiat has to go forth to shock mankind awake by the activities of Nature of which We are Master, the human beings of this world will want some Assistance!

Blessed Ones, We come to offer you Our Love! We have offered you the Sacred Fire! Whenever you think of the Sacred Fire, remember also to remind yourself, It is the Purifying Love of either the "Mighty I AM Presence" or the Ascended Host. The Angelic Host are the Beings who concentrate It, who call It forth from the Physical Sun and the Great Central Sun. We call It forth from Our Temples of the Sacred Fire in the Ascended Masters' Octave. Those Temples of the Sacred Fire are the Cosmic Concentration and Momentum of Our Life's Love that We have used down through the ages to create one magnificent manifestation after another that cannot do anything but bless Life and raise It into greater Perfection.

If the rest of mankind won't accept Our Presence and Our Reality, I come tonight to offer you again enough of the Sacred Fire's Purifying Love to be your Security against the hordes of evil; if you will remember Us, if you will associate with Us, if you will dwell with Us, if you will call to Us, if you will accept Our Presence with you, and if you will use the Love of the Sacred Fire which We bring to compel the Purification that must and shall dissolve and consume the hordes of evil mankind has created. So if you accept Us, We will be present with you! *(applause)* Thank you so much.

Now I am going to give you the Secret of Our Dwelling with you! If you want to see Us face to face with the outer sight, when you think of Our Visible, Tangible Presence, call to your "Beloved I AM Presence" to annihilate all human obstruction that keeps you from seeing Us—visible and tangible—at any time that We pour Our Love to you. *(applause)* Thank you so much. And at the same time, call to your "Beloved I AM Presence" and to Us to annihilate all obstruction in the atmosphere, not only all obstruction within your own mental and feeling world, but all obstruction in the atmosphere that keeps you from seeing Us face to face with the physical sight.

If you will make that Call, and you, with dynamic intensity, say to your "Beloved I AM Presence" and the Ascended Host: *"Annihilate every bit of obstruction in me and in the atmosphere around me that keeps me from seeing the Angelic Host who come to help me!"*–We can do It! Your "Presence" can do It! We have offered It down through the ages! We are the Annihilation of human obstruction! But you must arise in the Master Authority and Master Command of everything, every vibration of human creation within and around yourselves or in the atmosphere about you. Then when you say to your "Beloved I AM Presence," *"Purify me and annihilate everything within me that is an obstruction to my seeing the Angelic Host face to face! Annihilate in the atmosphere all that would be an obstruction, and blaze the Purity here in and around me that always lets me see Them–see the Angelic Host when They are pouring Love to me!"* My Dear Ones, We'll do It! We've promised, and there isn't a Promise We make that We can't fulfill!

Love is offering everything; but mankind does not want Purity, and Purity is imperative if individuals are going to see Us with the physical sight. So the day that you say to your "Presence" unconditionally: *"Blaze in, through, and around me whatever Sacred Fire Purity annihilates all obstruction in me and in the atmosphere around me that keeps me from seeing the 'Mighty I AM Presence' and the Ascended Host face to face!"*—the day you ask that, and the day you take your stand and demand it, your "Presence" and We will do it! So I offer you—*(long applause)* Thank you so much.

What do you think, Beloved Ones, would be the condition of mankind if individuals spent as much time calling for the Sacred Fire Purity of the "Mighty I AM Presence" and the Ascended Host to enable the outer self of each one, each Life Stream, to see the "Mighty I AM Presence" and the Ascended Host, as much time were spent on that as human beings spend watching the television or going to the moving pictures? What do you think would be the condition of the mankind of this world? They couldn't remain in their chains!—the people couldn't. Don't you see what people are doing with time? Don't you see what they are doing with energy? Don't you see what they are doing with the substance and the things of this world? The things they do with it enslave them to greater and greater destruction until the second death, and if they won't give into that thing, if they will call to Us, it will take them into the Ascension! Now people must decide what they want. They either want the "Mighty I AM Presence" and the Ascended Host's Purifying Love and the Victory of the Eternal Peace and Mastery of the Ascension or they do not. There is no compromise.

So long as human beings want the gratification of the physical senses and are not interested in Purity, then people's suffering goes on, and individuals go into greater and greater and greater destruction, until the second death is the result of it. Hordes of evil want to destroy you. Our Love wants to save not only you, but all mankind, all Life, from the experience of any more suffering produced by the hordes of evil. So when We come and have to beg to be accepted and beg to be recognized and beg to be understood—and We have to beg people to accept Our Love—which is Light and Purity and Happiness and Protection and Freedom for Eternity, what think you is the darkness that enfolds mankind?

Nobody can consume that but the Angelic Host and the "Mighty I AM Presence"! If Light doesn't come into the darkness, then the darkness destroys. So when it is necessary for Us to come and explain this and give this to you so you may use It; I am sure you recognize that the Mighty Saint Germain has called to Us for Assistance to be with you as much as possible, as much as you will call, and as much as you will let Us come near to you by the attention you give Us.

So Beloved Ones, in preparation for the Release of the Cosmic Light of a Thousand Suns, We want you enfolded in Our Angelic Host's Miracle Mantle of Sacred Fire Love's Mastery and Freedom from the hordes of evil. And surely you want that! *(applause)* Thank you so much. When mankind, masses of people, do not want the Love, the Purity, the Happiness, and the Freedom which We are and which We bring, there only lies ahead suffering, destruction, and torture.

Those of you who know this Law do not need to go through those experiences. If you should want to dispose of your problems or the mistakes you've made in the past, did it ever occur to you that Our Sacred Fire Purifying Love is the Annihilator and Preventor of all problems? Don't you understand that when you have human creation to deal with, and then the Cosmic Law of the Universe provides the Sacred Fire's Purifying Love to produce Perfection, then if there is something wrong here, then this Sacred Fire Purity must come here and consume it and replace it by Perfection! And if people will not understand it or will not do it, then there is nothing but torture ahead until they will. The Cosmic Law is Master regardless of who believes It or accepts It or not. Nobody breaks the Law! Individuals break themselves by disobedience to It, and all the denial on the Earth by all mankind can't take Us out of existence! *(applause)* Thank you so much. The darkness which has engulfed mankind and which has been generated by mankind contains nothing in it but torture and destruction and confusion. Until every particle of Life in existence turns to the "Beloved I AM Presence" and the Ascended Host, until the attention of Life goes to the Greater Life which is the Light of Love's Perfection; then if it will not turn to the Light, it will be destroyed by the darkness.

Beloved Ones, We come to redeem mankind. We come to bring Hope to those who are trying to hold to the constructive way of Life at this time. But We'll give no quarter to that which denies Us or defies Us or does not want Us. When individuals—whether it be one individual or many—want the Visible, Tangible Presence of the Angelic Host's Purifying Sacred Fire Love to come in and handle every condition in existence that mankind has generated; when individuals want that, the Great Cosmic Law is such that We have to give It. Your Blessed Saint Germain as Angel Deva of the Violet Flame has given and given and given the Love of that Violet Consuming Flame to harmoniously purify everything in existence. If mankind will understand It and use It; and remember, when you ask for Purification by the Violet Consuming Flame or Fiery Christ Blue Lightning Power or Force or Action, It is Love that purifies. That is the Gift of Love. That is the Mastery by which Love owns the Universe and is Master of Manifestation and is the Controller of every bit of energy in infinite space, and the mankind of this world is under the Control of that Law just the same as the Cosmic Suns throughout Creation.

So Blessed Ones, tonight I offer you the Master Presence of the Power Flame of the Angelic

Host's Purifying Sacred Fire Love that is enough to dissolve and consume the hordes of evil, the sinister force, the human creation that has been generated in this world and that has destroyed and desecrated the many Gifts that Love has given. Now Love must take Command of Its own, and those who will abide within It and dwell with Us will have Our Mastery surrounding them for survival and control in the midst of the destructive conditions the hordes of evil have generated. And I assure you, where We come to hold Protection, the hordes of evil will never abide! *(applause)* Thank you so much.

Now I have one more thing to say. There is no substitute for the Sacred Fire Love's Eternal Purity. All the intellectual consciousness in existence in mankind isn't a feather in a gust of wind compared to one Wave of Love from the Angelic Host that can cleanse the Earth in one Flash! What think you is the intellect of man unless it is the servant of the Love of the Heart, and obedient to the Cosmic Law which is embodied in Cosmic Beings who are that Love of Eternal Perfection? So when We wrap you in the Angelic Host's Miracle Mantle of the Sacred Fire Love's Victory over all in this world, It's no figment of anybody's imagination. It's a very Visible, Tangible Presence, and is Unconquerable Power! If you will accept It, We will give It! If you will use It, Its Power will expand around you!

And if you want Our Protection, We will be present with you, and you can see Us—visible with the physical sight and tangible—whenever you make the Call for the annihilation of all human obstruction within, and all human obstruction in the atmosphere about you. Then Our Presence will be with you wherever you want Us. May you remember this, and may We come quickly and show you that which is forever your Freedom. May the Mightiest Power of the Angelic Host's Purifying Love flash Its Flame everywhere in this city, everywhere in this Nation, everywhere in this world and its atmosphere, until the hordes of evil have been compelled to cease existence everywhere forever! And We shall never stop until that's accomplished. *(applause)* Thank you so much.

We enfold you in the Victory Power of Our Love and Its Blazing Presence that is a Light so Bright no human creation can exist for any reason whatsoever. Our Miracle Mantle of Love's Mastery is with you always; and in that Love We can come and forever raise you to the Great Perfection, and the Power and the Victory and the Mastery which We are everywhere throughout Creation for Eternity.

Thank you with all My Heart.

APPENDIX

REFERENCES TO ANGELS

February, 1936
through December, 1998

• SECTION ONE •
References to Angels in *"Voice of the I AM"*

• SECTION TWO •
References to Angels in the Books of
the Saint Germain Series

BELOVED ARCHANGEL MICHAEL
December 23, 1958
Record CD 535

Just imagine what would be your experience
if you contemplated the Angelic Host for one
whole hour. What do you think We could do for

you? Most of the time mankind only thinks of Us when individuals are in trouble, and then We're immediately forgotten as soon as the pathway is easy again. We'd like to reverse a little of that and be with you when the path is easy. It's more enjoyable for you and Us both! So now if you want to prove the Truth of My Words, contemplate Us in the midst of your daily work. You don't need to go woolgathering or sit in the corner or anything of the kind; but in the midst of your activity, for just the fraction of a second you can send your Flame of Love from your Heart—the Feeling of Love from your Heart—to the Angelic Host and thank Them for Their Love to this world. And if you recognize Their Love, more will come into you. One day you'll be like Them, and then you will understand how much mankind needs Their Love.

• SECTION ONE •

"Voice of the I AM," published by Saint Germain Press, is a monthly magazine of Ascended Master Words which were received through Mr. and Mrs. G. W. Ballard, Accredited Messengers of Beloved Saint Germain.

REFERENCE CATEGORIES

"VOICE OF THE I AM"
Abbreviations used:
    96.05   1996 issue, May

CASSETTE NUMBER
Numbering System:
    6_ _ _ _   Audio cassette tape number
Note: The code prefix for Dictation cassettes has been changed from "SGC" to "6" followed by as many zeros as it takes to make a five-digit number, including the original numbers. Example:
    SGC 12 is now 60012

    6_ _ _ _-2 signifies side 2

ASCENDED MASTER
DATE OF DICTATION

Audio cassettes and issues of *"Voice of the I AM"* are available through Saint Germain Press.

"VOICE OF THE I AM"	CASSETTE NUMBER	ASCENDED MASTER	DATE OF DICTATION
98.12		Ruler of Violet Planet	Aug 20, 61
98.12		Beloved Mary	Dec 24, 63
98.11		Beloved Saint Germain	May 12, 56
98.09		Ruler of the Violet Planet	Dec 30, 67
98.09		Elohim of Peace	Oct 31, 52
98.06		Beloved Ruler, Violet Planet	Sep 15, 62
98.04		Beloved Ruler, Violet Planet	Apr 12, 58
98.03		Beloved Arcturus	Jan 8, 66
98.01		Beloved Saint Germain	May 30, 63
97.09		Beloved God Tabor	Sep 24, 44
97.03		Beloved Jesus	April 6, 58
96.09	65114	Beloved Elohim of Peace	May 15, 50
96.08		Beloved Goddess of Peace	Jan 14, 55
96.07		Beloved Saint Germain	Aug 13, 39
96.06		Beloved Saint Germain	May 16, 50
96.05	60294-2	Beloved Archangel Michael	Aug 17, 70
96.03		Beloved Daddy/Godfre	May 3, 47
95.12		Beloved Saint Germain	Jul 25, 54
95.10		Beloved God Harmony	Nov 13, 38
95.01		Beloved Sanat Kumara	Sep 5, 53
94.11		Beloved Saint Germain	Sep 28, 47
94.07		Beloved Saint Germain	Jan 9, 44
94.01		Beloved Saint Germain	Feb 12, 45
93.12	65021	Beloved Jesus	Dec 25, 50
93.07		Beloved Elohim of Purity	Jan 16, 51
93.06		Beloved Saint Germain	Sep 30, 50

"VOICE OF THE I AM"	CASSETTE NUMBER	ASCENDED MASTER	DATE OF DICTATION
93.05		Messenger Number One	Jul 14, 52
93.01	60198-2	Beloved Sanat Kumara	May 25, 52
92.09		Beloved Goddess of Justice	Aug 18, 62
92.09		Beloved Saint Germain	Oct 24, 37
92.06		Beloved Goddess of Justice	Apr 26, 52
92.01		Beloved Saint Germain	Feb 22, 37
91.11		Beloved Jesus	Sep 20, 70
90.12		Beloved Polaris	Feb 9, 47
90.12		Beloved God Tabor	Dec 22, 38
90.11		Beloved Archangel Michael	Nov 24, 57
90.08		Beloved Diana	Jan 18, 55
90.07		Beloved Archangel Michael	Apr 27, 54
90.04		Beloved Lord Maha Chohan	Sep 2, 53
90.03		Beloved God Tabor	Feb 15, 45
90.02	60205-2	Beloved Saint Germain	Feb 23, 69
89.08		Beloved God Harmony	Apr 17, 50
89.06		Beloved Victory	May 20, 65
89.01		Beloved Victory	Nov 25, 48
88.12		Messenger Number One	Apr 29, 45
88.12		Beloved Saint Germain	Dec 27, 53
88.11	60050-2	Beloved God of Gold	Aug 18, 58
88.07		Beloved Cosmos	Sep 21, 53
88.06	65003	Beloved Cyclopea	Jan 19, 51
88.05		Beloved Victory	Jun 9, 51
88.03		Beloved Victory	Feb 17, 45
88.02	65002	Beloved Saint Germain	Jun 6, 51

"VOICE OF THE I AM"	CASSETTE NUMBER	ASCENDED MASTER	DATE OF DICTATION
88.02		Beloved Daddy	Sep 20, 45
87.09		Beloved Great Cosmic Angel	Sep 17, 58
87.09		Beloved Great Cosmic Angel	Sep 6, 53
87.08	60118-2	Beloved Elohim of Purity	Sep 8, 65
87.06		Beloved Sanat Kumara	Mar 9, 47
87.05		Angel Deva, Jade Temple	Jan 20, 51
87.04		Beloved Mary	Apr 20, 53
87.02		Beloved Saint Germain	Apr 12, 59
87.02		Beloved Daddy	Mar 8, 53
87.01		Beloved Saint Germain	Jan 10, 51
86.12		Beloved Victory	Sep 3, 53
86.09		Beloved Goddess of Liberty	Jul 4, 52
86.01	60125-2	Beloved Goddess of Liberty	May 10, 64
85.05		Beloved Mary	Apr 15, 45
85.01		Beloved Daddy	Jan 9, 44
84.11		Beloved Elohim of Peace	Mar 12, 50
84.08		Beloved Archangel Michael	Sep 2, 45
84.07		Beloved Goddess of Liberty	Oct 6, 38
84.01	60056-1	Beloved Great Cosmic Angel	Sep 13, 60
83.10		Beloved Saint Germain	Oct 3, 37
83.08		Beloved Lord Maitreya	Oct 2, 49
83.07		Beloved Goddess of Liberty	Feb 10, 50
83.06		Beloved Archangel Michael	Aug 13, 65
83.05	60143-1	Beloved Lady Master Nada	Aug 13, 57
82.10		Beloved Saint Germain	Nov 2, 44
81.08		Beloved Astrea	Aug 28, 47

"VOICE OF THE I AM"	CASSETTE NUMBER	ASCENDED MASTER	DATE OF DICTATION
81.06	60223-2	Beloved Victory	Aug 12, 54
81.03		Beloved Mary	Apr 17, 52
80.10		Beloved Arcturus	Jul 27, 47
80.09		Beloved God of Gold	Mar 21, 49
80.03		Beloved Rayborn, Mr.	Feb 13, 44
79.12		Beloved Mary	Feb 4, 45
79.11		Beloved Saint Germain	Nov 28, 46
79.07	60117	Beloved Daddy	Jun 30, 51
79.05		Beloved Goddess of Purity	Jan 28, 45
79.03		Beloved Jesus	Jun 25, 45
78.08		Beloved Elohim of Purity	May 21, 44
78.01		Beloved Victory	Nov 19, 59
78.01		Beloved Victory	Sep 16, 51
77.12		Beloved Saint Germain	May 20, 45
77.10		Beloved God Tabor	Jun 17, 44
77.08		Beloved K-17	Jul 29, 45
77.07		Beloved Great Cosmic Angel	May 21, 50
77.06		Beloved Ruler, Violet Planet	Apr 16, 55
77.06		Beloved Ruler, Violet Temple	Sep 13, 53
76.10		Beloved Lord Maitreya	Jan 14, 45
76.08		Beloved Goddess of Music	Sep 19, 58
76.04		Beloved Sanat Kumara	Mar 28, 48
76.03		Beloved Cha Ara	May 2, 50
76.02		Beloved Daddy	Feb 19, 50
76.02		Beloved Victory	Feb 23, 58
75.09		Beloved Leto	Jun 7, 44

"VOICE OF THE I AM"	CASSETTE NUMBER	ASCENDED MASTER	DATE OF DICTATION
75.05		Beloved Mary	May 14, 50
74.12	65013	Beloved Jesus	Jun 10, 51
74.10		Beloved Daddy	Mar 3, 49
74.09		Beloved Great Cosmic Angel	Sep 19, 52
74.04		Beloved Mary	Apr 1, 45
74.01		Beloved Archangel Michael	Feb 13, 52
73.11		Beloved Goddess of Justice	May 6, 45
73.10		Beloved Sanat Kumara	Sep 29, 57
73.09	65008	Beloved Venus	Jan 21, 51
73.05	60080	Beloved Archangel Michael	Sep 13, 51
73.01		Beloved Lady Master Nada	Apr 22, 45
72.12		Beloved Jesus	Jan 21, 45
72.08		Beloved Goddess of Music	Sep 21, 51
72.06		Beloved Lady Master Nada	Apr 19, 53
1953–1971		There were no *"Voice of the I AM"* publications from 1953 to 1971.	
52.12		Beloved Jesus	Aug 11, 53
52.09		Beloved Saint Germain	Apr 19, 69
52.08		Beloved Goddess of Light	May 2, 48
52.06		Beloved Archangel Michael	Jul 29, 45
52.05		Beloved Goddess of Purity	Jan 16, 44
52.04		Beloved Saint Germain	Oct 3, 70
52.03		Beloved Goddess of Justice	Jan 3, 70
52.02		Beloved God Tabor	Jul 25, 48

"VOICE OF THE I AM"	CASSETTE NUMBER	ASCENDED MASTER	DATE OF DICTATION
52.01	60259	Beloved Daddy	Oct 12, 69
51.11		Beloved Victory	Feb 11, 45
51.09		Beloved Lady Master Nada	Jun 1, 48
51.08		Beloved Jesus	Apr 9, 50
51.07		Beloved Victory	May 9, 44
51.06	60205-1	Beloved Saint Germain	Oct 3, 67
51.04		Beloved Saint Germain	Aug 13, 44
51.02		Beloved Elohim of Peace	Jul 8, 45
50.12		Beloved Elohim of Peace	Apr 1, 45
50.11		Beloved Saint Germain	Aug 10, 44
50.06		Beloved Rose of Light	Feb 4, 45
50.03	60111-1	Beloved Sanat Kumara	Aug 23, 51
50.01	60109-1	Beloved Sanat Kumara	Aug 13, 51
50.01	60108	Beloved Sanat Kumara	Aug 12, 51
49.07		Beloved Helios	May 4, 51
49.07		Beloved Helios	May 6, 51
49.06		Beloved Helios	May 2, 51
48.12		Beloved Great Cosmic Angel	Jan 9, 51
48.12	65016	Beloved Great Cosmic Angel	Jan 8, 51
48.12	65017	Beloved Great Cosmic Angel	Jan 7, 51
48.11		Beloved Great Cosmic Angel	Jan 6, 51
48.11		Beloved Great Cosmic Angel	Jan 5, 51
48.10	65011	Beloved Great Cosmic Angel	Jan 4, 51
48.10		Beloved Great Cosmic Angel	Jan 3, 51
48.09	65020	Beloved Great Cosmic Angel	Jan 2, 51
48.09		Beloved Great Cosmic Angel	Jan 1, 51

"VOICE OF THE I AM"	CASSETTE NUMBER	ASCENDED MASTER	DATE OF DICTATION
48.06		Beloved Jesus	Apr 4, 51
48.05		Beloved Jesus	Apr 3, 51
48.05		Beloved Jesus	Apr 2, 51
48.04		Beloved Jesus	Mar 31, 51
47.12	60113	Beloved Jesus	Sep 3, 51
47.12	60116-1	Beloved Saint Germain	Sep 2, 51
47.11	65005	Beloved Daddy	Jun 3, 5
47.09		Beloved Helios	Apr 30, 50
47.09		Beloved Helios	May 1, 50
47.06		Beloved Saint Germain	Oct 24, 49
47.05		Beloved Jesus	Aug 19, 49
47.03		Beloved Archangel Michael	Nov 24, 46
46.08		Beloved Lord Maha Chohan	May 20, 45
45.10		Beloved Saint Germain	Jan 21, 44
45.09		Beloved Archangel Michael	May 6, 45
45.07		Beloved Daddy	Feb 11, 45
45.05		Beloved Helios	Feb 6, 45
45.04		Beloved Mary	Aug 15, 44
45.03		Beloved Virgo	Feb 18, 45
45.01		Beloved Saint Germain	Nov 30, 44
45.01		Beloved Goddess of Justice	Jan 23, 44
44.12		Beloved Jesus	May 18, 44
44.12		Beloved Mary	Mar 5, 44
44.11		Beloved Hope	Apr 16, 44
44.10		Angel Deva, Jade Temple	Jul 23, 44
44.06		Beloved Leto	Jan 12, 44

"VOICE OF THE I AM"	CASSETTE NUMBER	ASCENDED MASTER	DATE OF DICTATION
44.05		Beloved Elohim of Peace	Mar 19, 44
44.04		Beloved Goddess of Music	Jan 20, 44
44.04		Beloved Jesus	Apr 9, 44
44.03		Beloved Goddess of Music	Jan 16, 44
44.02		Beloved Daddy	Jan 30, 44
44.01		Beloved Saint Germain	Jan 13, 44
44.01		Beloved Daddy	Jan 7, 44
43.12		Beloved Jesus	Nov 25, 37
41.11		Beloved Sanat Kumara	Jul 26, 37
41.06		Beloved Lanto	Jun 24, 37
40.09		Beloved Cuzco	Jul 25, 39
40.01		Beloved Goddess of Music	Dec 4, 39
39.12		Beloved Great Divine Director	Oct 22, 39
39.11		Beloved Goddess of Purity	Oct 1, 39
39.10		Beloved Ray-O-Light	Sep 10, 39
39.09		Beloved Eriel	Jul 23, 39
39.01		Beloved Saint Germain	Dec 29, 38
38.07		Beloved Goddess of Peace	May 19, 38
38.05		Beloved Lady Master Nada	Mar 29, 38
37.08		Beloved Saint Germain	Jun 25, 37
37.07		Beloved Great Divine Director	Jun 9, 37
37.03		Beloved Lady Master Nada	Jan 14, 37
37.01		Beloved Saint Germain	Nov 16, 36
36.10		Beloved Saint Germain	Aug 2, 36
36.10		Beloved Saint Germain	Aug 31, 36
36.08		Beloved Oromasis	Jun 25, 36

· SECTION TWO ·

The fifteen Books of the Saint Germain Series, published by Saint Germain Press, gives the Ascended Master Instruction in Its pure, unadulterated form, free from any human interpretation, personal monetary gain, or proselytizing, as It is a Gift from the Great Ascended Masters and Cosmic Beings to bring Illumination and Perfection to mankind.

REFERENCE CATEGORIES

VOLUME

    Abbrevations used:

        Note: Volume 9 of the Saint Germain Series contains two sections, Part 1 and Part 2 and is referenced as follows:

            9-1   Volume 9, part 1

            9-2   Volume 9, part 2

CHAPTER

ASCENDED MASTER

DATE OF DICTATION

Books of the Saint Germain Series are available through Saint Germain Press.

VOLUME	CHAPTER	ASCENDED MASTER	DATE OF DICTATION
3	4	Beloved Saint Germain	Oct 13, 32
3	29	Beloved Arcturus	Aug 19, 34
4	3	Beloved Saint Germain	Jun 11, 32
4	11	Beloved Saint Germain	Aug 8, 32
4	12	Beloved Saint Germain	Aug 11, 32
4	14	Beloved Saint Germain	Aug 18, 32
4	28	Beloved Arcturus	Aug 19, 34
6	1	Beloved Saint Germain	Jan 1, 37
6	8	Beloved Arcturus	Mar 21, 37
7	5	Beloved Sanat Kumara	Jul 11, 37
7	15	Beloved God Tabor	Jun 27, 37
7	16	Beloved God Himalaya	Jun 27, 37
7	25	Beloved David Lloyd	Mar 4, 38
8	4	Great Divine Director	Apr 21, 37
8	7	Great Divine Director	Jun 7, 37
8	21	Great Divine Director	Aug 21, 38
9-2	1	Beloved Victory	Nov 5, 44
9-2	3	Beloved Victory	Nov 19, 44
9-2	5	Beloved Victory	Dec 3, 44
9-2	6	Beloved Victory	Dec 10, 44
11	1	Beloved Saint Germain	Oct 24, 37
11	10	Beloved Saint Germain	Oct 9, 38

THE SAINT GERMAIN
SERIES